GI

- Three tips for enhancing your work space—even in an open area
- Rules for success in dealing with a supervisor
- Guidelines for overseeing temporary workers, student interns, or new employees
- The chart that gives you the leading edge when working for a promotion
- The efficiency techniques that really work for doing a first-rate job . . . on time
- What every employee and supervisor needs to know about sexual harassment
- Nonsexist terminology that is gender neutral for all written or spoken correspondence
- Expert tips for successful filing
- What you need to watch for in office-equipment service contracts
- A handy guide to purchasing office supplies . . . and much more

FILLED WITH INFORMATION YOU WILL USE EVERY DAY, THE *21ST CENTURY OFFICE ASSISTANT'S MANUAL* IS DESIGNED TO PRODUCE OUTSTANDING PERFORMANCE AND EXCELLENCE IN TODAY'S HIGHLY DEMANDING BUSINESS ENVIRONMENT.

21ST CENTURY
OFFICE ASSISTANT'S MANUAL

21st Century Office Assistant's Manual

Edited by the Princeton Language Institute

K.A. Zahler, Compiler

Ellen Lichtenstein, Editor

Produced by The Philip Lief Group, Inc.

A LAUREL BOOK

Published by
Dell Publishing
a division of
Bantam Doubleday Dell Publishing Group, Inc.
1540 Broadway
New York, New York 10036

Published by arrangement with The Philip Lief Group, Inc
6 West 20th Street
New York, New York 10011

ISBN: 0-440-21725-3

Printed in the United States of America

Published simultaneously in Canada

January 1996

10 9 8 7 6 5 4 3 2 1

21ST CENTURY OFFICE ASSISTANT'S MANUAL

Contents

Figures and Illustrations

I

Duties and Rights

1

Types of Offices

- Formal *vs.* Informal Offices
- Traditional Corporations
- Small Businesses
- Office Layout and Ergonomics
- Dealing with the Public
- Specialization
- Certification
- Safety on the Job
- Alternatives to 9-to-5 Work
- Reward Systems and Retirement Benefits

Every office has its own structure, its own tempo, its own personality. Once you've landed your office job, you begin a training process that has nothing to do with upgrading your keyboarding skills. You need to learn the ins and outs of your particular office—who reports to whom, what behavior is required, how much work is demanded of you in how little time—what you can expect of your company and what your company will expect of you. This can take weeks, even months to learn, but your success and happiness in your new job depend on your understanding the unique character of your office.

FORMAL VS. INFORMAL OFFICES

Careful observation at your opening interview will probably tell you important things about your new environment. Is there a receptionist? How is he or she dressed? Are you ushered into a comfortable room to await your meeting or are you left waiting in the hallway? Is your interview with a personnel director, a human resources professional, or your immediate supervisor-to-be?

The larger a company, the more formal the atmosphere is likely to be; a Fortune 500 company will generally require more formal dress and decorum than a five-person firm. Like all rules, however, this one has exceptions. An office in a sprawling university complex or in a high-tech company may feature workers in very casual attire, while a small-sized insurance office might have a conservative dress code.

Traditionally, businesses with especially formal requirements include banking and finance, insurance, real estate, and law. Other professions offer a more relaxed atmosphere: publishing is less formal than law; advertising is less formal than banking.

The formality of an office goes beyond dress. Often, a formal-appearing work environment indicates formality in regulations and practices as well. A formal place of business is more likely to require a probationary period when you are first hired, to have salary reviews and job performance evaluations, and to have a rigid chain of command (see Chapter 2). An informal office will have rules, too, but they are often more relaxed.

Don't prejudge your ability to work in an unfamiliar work environment. For example, if you're used to working in a casual atmosphere, you may welcome the structure that a formal office brings to your labor. You may do your best work in a strictly regulated environment. Alternatively, your less formal ways of working, as long as they do not interfere with the habits of others in the office, may be a breath of fresh air and serve to convince your employers that you are creative and original. Do not, however, leap right in and shake things up. You need to prove yourself before you *slowly* adjust your environment to suit your needs.

If you are moving from a formal work situation to an informal one, the change in atmosphere may be dizzying at first. Again, it is a mistake to leap in and try to change things. Your employer does not need to hear that your last company did things in a saner and more organized manner. Once you have made some adjustments of your own, you can *slowly* begin to suggest alternatives to the chaos you see around you.

TRADITIONAL CORPORATIONS

Traditionally, large corporations functioned in a paternalistic role. The company took care of its workers, providing benefits such as health insurance, housing loans, moving allowances, credit unions, free annual medical checkups, college scholarships, and so on. Many of today's large and global corporations still provide excellent benefits, but the monolithic nature of these companies may eliminate the comfort level that workers once had—the feeling that the corporation knew them personally and would take personal care of them throughout their working lives.

Despite this change in attitude, the diversity and benefits available in a large company can be very attractive. If you find yourself unhappy in one division, you might transfer your skills to another division where you are more comfortable. The larger the staff, the greater your chances for promotion. In addition, large companies are more likely to have the money to buy the computer you want, send you to a seminar, or pay for your schooling.

SMALL BUSINESSES

Small businesses can provide growth opportunities lacking in larger companies. Drawbacks can include lower salaries and longer working hours, especially for startup businesses. Nevertheless, the pluses may be good for your career.

You may end up with far more responsibility than you would as an office assistant in a large company, simply because there are not as many people to take on all the office duties. Working for a small company may enable you to learn more skills more quickly than working for a large corporation. This is especially true if your company is relatively young; there is nothing more exciting than "getting in on the ground floor" with a new business and being a part of that company's growth and success.

OFFICE LAYOUT AND ERGONOMICS

With space at a premium, more and more companies are knocking down walls and hiring experts to design partitions that maximize usable floorspace and allow for more employees per square foot.

As any alumnus of an open classroom can attest, it's hard to work in an exposed environment. The noise level alone can be distracting, and the constant parade of people walking by can keep the most determined worker from attending to the task at hand.

Here are some helpful guidelines:

Move your desk to face a wall or window. This helps cut down on peripheral distractions.

Observe "traffic patterns"; make phone calls or meet with people at the height of the traffic. Save tasks that involve concentration for quiet times.

If company rules allow it, play a radio softly. Don't use earphones—they'll drown everything out—but a quiet "white noise" effect from a radio may help you filter out background din.

Ergonomics is a scientific application of the principles of engineering and biology to problems relating to people and machinery. Do straightback chairs hurt your back when you type all day? Try an ergonomically designed knee-rest chair. Is your carpal tunnel syndrome caused by repeated motions at the keyboard? Ergonomists experiment with raising and lowering chairs and desks, tilting keyboards, separating keys, and so on. Do workers in your building suffer respiratory ailments due to "Sick Building Syndrome"? Perhaps it's time to install an ergonomically sound air-filtration system.

Your own brief "ergonomic" study can help you improve your work center. Run through this checklist.

Ergonomic Checklist

- Look straight ahead. Can you see at a glance everything you need to see?
- Can you stand up without hitting your head on a shelf or overhang?
- Is your chair comfortable? Can you cross your legs? How does your back feel at the end of the day?
- Can you reach your phone/books/ word processor without having to stand up or scoot your chair across the floor?
- If someone needs to meet with you, do you have to move to a different room?

Fig. 1.1

Use the results of your "study" to make some changes. Can you realign your desk to give yourself a better view of things?

Can you remove obstacles or reorganize objects to avoid hazards? Can you requisition a better chair or trade with someone else? Can you rearrange your desk so that everything is within reach? Can you make room for an extra chair or stool so that someone else can join you in your workspace? It doesn't take a scientific engineer to see that a few simple changes can make your work life a great deal easier.

DEALING WITH THE PUBLIC

Does your position require you to interact with people rather than co-workers? Do you fill in for the receptionist when he or she goes to lunch? Do visitors notice you when they come in for appointments? Working directly in the public eye can be fun, but it demands poise and flexibility.

Clients requesting information should not be kept waiting while you attend to copying duties. Telephone callers should not be put on hold several times while you deal with face-to-face inquiries. You must learn how to balance different tasks by paying close attention to the way your office works. Do you get a lot of face-to-face traffic at certain times of day? Put off your duties that require concentration until the traffic slows down. If necessary, ask your boss to prioritize your work. Make sure you know which tasks are most vital and which can wait until after you have dealt with the public. (See chapter 3.)

Remember, you make an impression when you are in the public eye. Dress and act accordingly.

SPECIALIZATION

Certain offices require special skills. An office worker trained in general office work may need additional training to work in one of these specialized positions. On the other hand, office assistants who learn the skills, vocabulary, and techniques specific to these particular positions will find themselves in great demand, and will receive a higher salary than office assistants elsewhere.

Specialized Job Skills

legal assistant	writing, proofreading, knowledge of legal vocabulary
medical assistant	scheduling, accounting, claims processing, performing clinical tasks, knowledge of medical vocabulary
nonprofit agency assistant	scheduling, fundraising, bulk mailing, preparing grant requests
research assistant	editing, proofreading, knowledge of math and science, preparing grant requests, knowledge of technical vocabulary

Fig. 1.2

CERTIFICATION

You can become a certified secretary, legal secretary, or medical assistant by meeting certain educational requirements and passing standardized tests. Some offices require certification of their workers, and without a doubt, certification can lead to promotion and higher pay. (For more information, see List of Resources on page 309.)

SAFETY ON THE JOB

It is your right to feel safe in your place of business. Now that the smallest operation often houses computers and other expensive equipment, burglary is a major concern. Businesses are fighting back with complex access control systems. At the time of your initial employment, you may be issued a key or a keycard that enables you to enter your building or floor. You may be given a badge or photo identification card that you must wear as you move around the building. You may be asked to memorize a code and to enter that code on a keypad each time you enter or leave. All of this may combine to make you feel restricted and confined, but it is better than the alternative. If you want safety, you must put up with a little aggravation. In the 21st century, we can expect even more sophisticated access control, perhaps using fingerprints or voice prints, as are now used in some restricted government buildings.

If your office is *not* secure, bring this to the attention of the people in charge. Your local police or sheriff's department will be glad to do a safety assessment for your organization and make recommendations about how to improve security.

ALTERNATIVES TO 9-TO-5 WORK

Some forward-thinking businesses are meeting the needs of their employees and strengthening themselves by presenting alternatives to the standard workday and/or work week. Some options that you might be offered are flex-time, part-time work, job sharing, or a compressed work week.

Flex-time options usually give workers a variety of possible daily schedules. Worker A might work from 8 until 4, while Worker B works from noon until 8 at night. This kind of flexibility has been shown to reduce absenteeism significantly. It takes advantage of the fact that some people are morning people, and others function best later in the day. It is up to you to be aware of which hours you are most productive.

Part-time jobs have always existed, but many corporations are now providing part-time work as an alternative to layoffs or as a way for new parents to ease back into the work force. Part-time employment enables workers to spend more time with family and tasks outside the office; however, companies need not offer part-time workers the same benefits as full-time employees.

Job sharing is a recent phenomenon that is proving very popular. Two workers "share" the traditional 40-hour work week, splitting it up in one of several ways. This system may again be used as an alternative to layoffs or as a boon for new parents, but often serves as a way for a couple (married or not) to work in the same environment or for two unrelated workers to pursue individual outside interests (school, volunteer work, or artistic endeavors, for example) while continuing to receive a paycheck. Worker A might work mornings while Worker B works afternoons, or Worker A might work Monday through Wednesday while Worker B works Thursday and Friday. Job sharing is as flexible as the company that provides it; it may be a temporary or a permanent arrangement.

Compressed work weeks mean that employees work the standard 40-hour week in fewer than five business days. This allows workers to balance home and work while employers maintain full productivity.

More and more alternatives will be developed as companies face the demands of the 21st century. Some companies may ask you to work seven-day weeks in return for time off at some later date. Some workers may find that temporary, or temp work, which enables them to earn a good paycheck while moving around from job to job, suits them better than the routine of working for one company. The options are out there, but you may need to shop around to find the alternative that suits your needs.

REWARD SYSTEMS AND RETIREMENT BENEFITS

Having learned valuable lessons from companies overseas, our own corporations are turning toward pay-for-performance strategies and incentives that, in some cases, make workers part owners of their companies. Companies have also instituted different plans to help employees save money for their retirement.

Bonuses are a fairly traditional way of rewarding performance. Companies return a percentage of profits to those employees whose labor has increased production. Unfortunately, bonuses in many companies are restricted to executives, but this is changing; research shows that incentives like this increase productivity and more than pay for themselves.

Profit sharing is one kind of long-term retirement plan. Employees are generally informed on a regular basis about the company's profits and losses, just as though they were stockholders. Employers contribute a percentage of the company's profits, either at a flat rate, or on a sliding scale.

Stock purchase programs allow workers to own a percentage of the business in the form of common stock. ESOPs (employee stock ownership plans) are one form of stock purchase program. Employees buy stock in the company and have standard stockholders' voting rights on the direction the company will take. When they retire or leave the company, they cash out their stock distributions. Some ESOPs allow workers to cash out in times of need—for a child's college tuition, for example. In extreme cases, stock is sold with the expectation that the workers will end up owning the company.

401(k)s or salary deferral plans allow employees to defer amounts that would otherwise be included in salary on a pretax basis. The money is invested, and income tax is deferred on the contribution and its earnings until retirement.

Money purchase plans are retirement plans in which the

benefits at retirement depend on the performance of the company's investments.

Thrift plans encourage workers to be thrifty by donating matching employer contributions to a retirement fund for each dollar contributed by the worker.

Many offices are beginning to provide alternatives in benefit packages as well. You may be asked to choose from an assortment of benefit plans, or you might be given a set amount of money to apply toward your coverage. If you prefer an HMO to standard health insurance, you may have that choice. If your partner's insurance already covers you, you may be able to return the money and apply it to salary. Expect more variety in benefit packages as the 21st century begins.

2

Office Politics

- Business Hierarchies
- Working with Management
- Working with Subordinates
- When the Boss Is Away
- Formal Information Networks
- Informal Information Networks
- Appropriate Dress
- Appropriate Behavior
- Appropriate Speech
- Getting Noticed
- Mentors
- Up the Ladder

Every place of business has its own hierarchy of power based on who reports to whom. One of the first things you must do when you start a new job is determine who is in charge of whom. Who is your supervisor? Who is her or his supervisor? Who makes what decisions? How much decision-making power do *you* have?

BUSINESS HIERARCHIES

To divide up the labor involved in a business, it is necessary to have levels of workers. Most businesses have a pyramid structure like the following example:

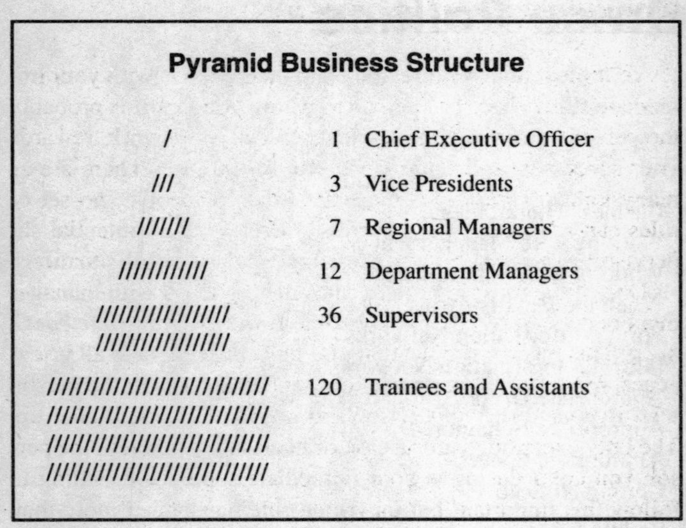

Fig. 2.1

The above business is somewhat more clear-cut than most businesses in which you are likely to work. Here, each trainee and assistant reports to one of 36 supervisors. Each supervisor reports to one of 12 department managers, who report to one of seven regional managers, and so on up the pyramid.

In the example above, every worker at a given level would have the same responsibilities and the same salary as every other worker at that level. In fact, most businesses are much more complicated than that. Responsibility and salary are often based on how long you have worked for a business. An office assistant who is new to the job cannot expect the same level of responsibility as one who has been with the firm five years. In addition to seniority, your education, training, and previous job experience may define the scope of your responsibilities.

WORKING WITH MANAGEMENT

Your most important relationship on the job is with your immediate supervisor. The person to whom you report is probably the person who sets your agenda, reviews your work, rewards your successes, and reprimands you for failures. There are as many kinds of bosses as there are kinds of people; no set of rules can adequately prepare you to deal with all potential supervisors. These rules, however, apply to nearly all situations.

One of the most important rules having to do with management and chain of command is this: *Don't go over your boss's head.* This means, simply, that you must initially take all grievances, requests, recommendations, and proposals to the person who is your direct supervisor and not to someone higher up. The only exception is for a case of harassment wherein the person you are accusing is your immediate supervisor. Failing to follow this important but unwritten rule has landed more than one eager employee in serious trouble.

During times of need, you may find yourself being lent out to another manager. Make sure to have your new responsibilities defined so that both your supervisors and you understand and agree to them.

Dealing with Your Supervisor

1. *Understand deadline pressures.* Any supervisor can be extremely sensitive when faced with approaching deadlines. The boss who usually chats with you during your break may suddenly chastise you for taking a break at all. Don't take it personally.
2. *Ask questions.* It is always better to confess ignorance than to forge ahead blindly with a task you do not understand. Sometimes you can get the information you need from your peers. Most of the time you're better off asking your boss.
3. *Apologize.* You're going to make mistakes; everyone does. Admit it, say you're sorry, and move on.
4. *Be a team player.* Your ideas may be brilliant, but your supervisor may not always think so. Worse, your boss may pass off your ideas as his or her own. It rankles, but your time will come. You are part of a team, and if there is any star player, it's your supervisor, not you—yet. Do keep written records of your significant contributions, as they will aid you in moving up the ladder and/or in getting raises.

Fig. 2.2

WORKING WITH SUBORDINATES

Often, office assistants find themselves in charge of other employees—a stable of temporary workers during a deadline crunch, a group of student interns over the summer, or new assistants who must be trained. The following guidelines will help you in your supervisory capacity.

Dealing with Office Help

1. *Talk to your supervisor.* Make sure you and your supervisor agree on the extent of your responsibilities. Does your boss want reports from you on their work, or are you solely in charge? How much of your time should be dedicated to overseeing? Must you find things for the workers to do, or will their work be assigned by your supervisor?
2. *Delegate.* Now that you have help, use it! Assess each worker's ability, and assign tasks that you think they can handle. Review their work regularly. See Chapter 3, page 32, for tips on this important skill.
3. *Make yourself available.* Recognize that new workers will need help. In order to avoid spending all your time supervising, you might meet with them at set times of the day.

Fig. 2.3

Your ability to supervise others may be watched by manage-ent and used as a means of judging whether you deserve a omotion. Think about the best boss you ever had. What made at boss great? List her or his good qualities and try to develop ose qualities in yourself.

HEN THE BOSS IS AWAY

Depending on the hierarchy in your place of business, you y find yourself in a position of authority when your boss is ay. Managers often rely on their assistants to keep things nning smoothly during their absence. You can earn a lot of nts with management if you prove that you can do profes-nal, courteous, and efficient work without your supervisor re to direct you.

Make sure these items have been cleared in advance with your supervisor.

- Will he or she call in daily? At what time?
- Will you allow phone messages to pile up, or will you be expected to deal with certain issues on your own? Which issues?
- Will you be responsible for overseeing anyone else?
- Can you set up appointments or meetings for your supervisor for the time when she or he returns, or should all such scheduling be postponed until that time?
- May you give out your supervisor's number to anyone? To whom?

If your supervisor does not schedule a meeting with you before her or his departure, schedule the meeting yourself. Clearing these issues in advance will ensure a smooth transition over the time your supervisor is away, and you will feel comfortable and confident as you go about both your businesses.

FORMAL INFORMATION NETWORKS

All office workers should stay informed about their companies. Be aware of events in other departments or on other floors. The more you know, the more useful you can be to your department, to your boss, and to yourself. Larger companies oft[en] have several formal means of circulating information. Ev[en] small companies may use one or more of these methods.

Annual reports are year-end financial documents meant f[or] individual and institutional shareholders, but they can be a go[od] source of information for staff members as well.

House organs are often sophisticated and glossy compa[ny] publications distributed to staff, salespeople, and custome[rs]. They may be published monthly, bi-monthly, or quarterly.

Newsletters are less sophisticated than house organs. They may be published within a single division of the company on a weekly or monthly basis.

Memos are everpresent in offices; on any given day, you probably prepare more than one and see dozens. Anyone can send a memo, and many people send them instead of convening meetings or using the telephone. It's tempting to ignore this flood of paper, but memos can be the single most important source of information available to you. Read every memo sent to you directly. Memos that note rules or regulation changes should be kept in a notebook for ready reference. If you feel you should be included on a memo distribution list, inform your supervisor.

INFORMAL INFORMATION NETWORKS

Large or small, all offices have informal ways of circulating information. Watch the bulletin board to see what jobs are opening in which departments; this gives you an idea of who's moving up, who's moving out, and where the action is. Use the grapevine to your advantage. Have lunch with the people in your department; you're sure to learn something you may need to know. Have lunch with people outside your department; you can share information (as long as it's not confidential) and find out what's happening outside your little niche. Use your powers of observation and social skills wisely to become an informed employee.

A warning about gossip: It can backfire. First of all, it can be untrue. You may report back to your supervisor that an individual is leaving the company only to later learn that that same person is taking over your very division. Second, gossip may be paralyzing. In times of layoffs or reorganization, rumor breeds rumor, and employees may end up doing little *but* gossiping—speculating on who might be dismissed, who might buy the company, whose salaries might be cut, whose positions might be eliminated. This kind of gossip gets you nowhere; it feeds on itself and ends up occupying too much of your time. A smart company will nip this in the bud by alerting workers to new realities as soon as possible.

APPROPRIATE DRESS

Books have been written about dressing for success. The most useful rule is to observe those around you, especially your supervisor. If you wish to move up in a company, the standard maxim states that you should dress like the people on the level above yours. This doesn't mean that you should wear expensive suits if you can't afford them. Moderation is the key; you can look perfectly neat and professional on a small budget.

Every office is different. Some offices thrive on informality. Even in these offices, however, you should observe a certain amount of restraint. The respect you are given will correspond to the clothes you wear—it sounds unfair, but it is true. If you dress like a student, you will be treated like a student. If you dress like a manager, you will be treated like a manager.

APPROPRIATE BEHAVIOR

Just as correct dress will vary from place to place, so will correct behavior. Moderation, again, is the key, and these rules are practically universal.

Office Behavior Don'ts

Do not:

- Arrive late for work or meetings
- Smoke in a non-smoking area
- Spend too much time on personal phone calls
- Use your supervisor's office unless invited
- Criticize your boss or your company
- Drink too much at lunch or office parties
- Pass off someone's ideas as your own
- Blame others for your mistakes

Fig. 2.4

The Golden Rule is a good guideline for behavior on the job: Do unto others as you would have them do unto you. Excessive noise is rude, excessive lateness is rude, excessive familiarity or disrespect is rude. If your own boss is rude, make it your goal to be ultra-polite to counterbalance that rudeness. Others in your company are probably aware of your boss's disposition and will thank you for refusing to descend to his or her level.

APPROPRIATE SPEECH

Most jobs require you to have good oral communication skills. Ask yourself:

How's my diction? Do you enunciate your words clearly? If English is not your first language, you may need practice, but even native speakers often slur their speech or speak too quickly or too monotonously to be well understood. A tape recorder can be a powerful ally in improving your diction. Read something aloud into the recorder. Then spend two minutes telling the recorder about your day at work. Play it back. Is your diction clear when you read aloud? Does it become less clear when you improvise? Practice daily until you are satisfied with your performance.

How's my vocabulary? Having a good command of the English language means knowing how to use words effectively. A strong vocabulary is an important asset in business. You can improve your skills by reading and studying.

How's my tone? Do you turn high-pitched and squeaky when you're upset? Does your voice sound nasal? If so, use your tape recorder to smooth out your tone. Practice speaking from the diaphragm rather than from the front of your head or the back of your throat. Use a sound device such as a tuning fork to try lowering your normal speaking voice a few tones.

How's my sensitivity? Office workers today are usually required to write in non-sexist language. You should try to speak that way as well. (Refer to chapter 10 for a discussion of "Nonsexist Terminology." Profanity and vulgarity also have no place in an office. If you offend others with insensitive speech, you damage your own position in the company.

GETTING NOTICED

A certain amount of self-promotion is necessary if you want your talents to be appreciated and rewarded. Make sure that memos you produce yourself have your name on them. If a project is running late, volunteer your services, making sure to explain just what special aptitude you can bring to the effort. Offer to take on certain unwanted tasks: preparing the staff newsletter, for example, or labeling slides for a presentation.

Does your office have a favorite charity? Volunteer to run the holiday fund drive. Does your office have a softball team? Try out. Can you join a professional organization or take a class that will help you to advance your skills? Make sure your boss knows about it. Time and unpaid effort are needed to build a career, but the effort you put forth now will be rewarded once your name and abilities are more widely known. In addition to improving your chances for promotion, you will learn a great deal about how your company works.

MENTORS

Another way of gaining recognition is to attach yourself to a successful sponsor or mentor. Your mentor is most likely to be your boss, but it might be the person who recommended your hiring or a long-term employee who has charitably decided to take you under his or her wing.

A mentor will provide you with information, advice, and warnings. You can learn the customs of your company much faster with a mentor to guide you. A mentor in a position of real power can help your career take off. However, not everyone is meant to be a mentor, and not everyone deserves to have a mentor. Many workers are too insecure or self-involved to offer free counsel to a new employee. On the other hand, latching on to someone simply because she or he may benefit your career is almost guaranteed to fail. A mentor relationship involves give-and-take. It is mutually beneficial; it provides satisfaction to the mentor as well as assistance to the person being educated.

UP THE LADDER

At some point in your career, you will consider your position in the chain of command. Do you want more responsibility, or are you satisfied where you are?

When you are making this evaluation, you will need to be familiar with your company's operation and the levels of workers within the company. If you decide to make a move, you must compare your skills and knowledge to the requirements of the job you want. Make a chart like this one.

Job Comparison Chart

The Job I Have	The Job I Want
title: ________	________
salary: ________	________
benefits: ________	________
________	________
skills needed: ________	________
________	________
________	________
________	________
responsibilities: ________	________
________	________
________	________
________	________
advantages: ________	________
________	________
disadvantages: ________	________
________	________

Fig. 2.5

Take a close look at your chart. Do you have the skills needed to do the job you want? What additional skills must you acquire? Can you handle the responsibilities of the new job? What will be hard for you? What will be easy?

Compare the advantages and disadvantages and weigh them. Does the advantage of a higher salary outweigh the disadvantage of having to travel twice a month? Does the advantage of more recognition outweigh the disadvantage of less free time? Even if you feel completely content in your work, it's a good idea to shake yourself up every six months by charting your job satisfaction. You may well find that the job you have *is* the one you want, but you may also discover areas where you can add some skills, ask for more responsibility, improve yourself, and increase your value to your employer.

3

Managing Time

- A Typical Day
- Your Daily Agenda
- Learning to Delegate
- Creative Problem Solving
- A Place for Everything
- Deadline Pressure
- Seasonal Pressure
- Homework

Around the turn of the century, engineer and author Frederick Winslow Taylor introduced time-and-motion study to American businesses. Suddenly, companies were flooded with "experts" in laboratory coats, brandishing stopwatches and churning out reports on how to eliminate wasted time by minimizing movement.

Although few of us go as far as the Taylorists did, we still worry about using our time efficiently. There are a number of things you can do to learn to manage your time. Some are scientific, but most rely on plain old common sense.

A TYPICAL DAY

Think about your typical day at work. How many tasks do you begin and never finish? How often are you interrupted? How do you use your most productive time? How do you use those small chunks of time between meetings or before breaks?

Prepare a task-management chart for your use. Fill it in on a typical work day to analyze your use of time.

Task-Management Chart

task: ______ begun: __ : __ finished? ___ if so, when? __ : __
interrupted? ___ if so, by whom? __________

task: ______ begun: __ : __ finished? ___ if so, when? __ : __
interrupted? ___ if so, by whom? __________

task: ______ begun: __ : __ finished? ___ if so, when? __ : __
interrupted? ___ if so, by whom? __________

task: ______ begun: __ : __ finished? ___ if so, when? __ : __
interrupted? ___ if so, by whom? __________

task: ______ begun: __ : __ finished? ___ if so, when? __ : __
interrupted? ___ if so, by whom? __________

task: ______ begun: __ : __ finished? ___ if so, when? __ : __
interrupted? ___ if so, by whom? __________

Fig. 3.1

Your completed chart will show you where your time-management problems lie. Are you constantly interrupted by the same person? Do morning tasks drag over into the afternoon? How many jobs were left unfinished at the end of the day? Which jobs were they?

YOUR DAILY AGENDA

You can make inroads into your time-management problems by working from a daily agenda. It can be as rigid or casual as you and your particular office need. Here are three sample agendas for workers performing the same jobs:

Sample Agendas

AGENDA FOR WORKER A	AGENDA FOR WORKER B
Thursday, November 11	To do Thursday:
9–9:30 phone all clients to remind about meet-ing next week	phone clients*
9:30–10 correspondence	type letters
10–10:15 break	meet with Mr. X*
11–12 prepare documents	work in reception*
12–1 lunch	staff meeting*
1–1:30 assist receptionist	copying
1:30–2 meet with Mr. X	filing
2–2:30 staff meeting	
2:30–4 prepare documents	
4–5:30 copy and file	

AGENDA FOR WORKER C

11/11

1 phone clients	meetings:	Mr. X (1:30) staff (2:00)
3 type correspondence		
2 input documents	other:	sub for receptionist (1:00)
4 copy documents		
5 file manuscripts		

Fig. 3.2

All three workers have the same tasks to complete. To enable her to guarantee that everything gets done, Worker A outlines her day by time period. Of course, if something out of the ordinary happens, it may throw her schedule off.

Worker B lists all the day's jobs in no particular order and then puts an asterisk next to those that *must* be attended to. He has assigned a priority to preparing documents but not to typing letters. He is likely to begin with his most important tasks and save the others for the end of the day.

On the left of her agenda, Worker C records all tasks for the day, and on the right, she lists all meetings and other required events with their starting times. Then she ranks the tasks on the left in order of priority. This gives her a good idea as to what to do first, second, third, and so on. On Friday, tasks that remain unfinished will appear on a new agenda, and their ranks may change depending on what additional tasks are required on Friday.

No matter what kind of agenda you use, you must learn to classify your daily tasks in terms of urgency. Many people waste too much time on trivial duties or on "fun," creative tasks at the expense of essential ones. At first, your boss can help you decide which of your duties take precedence, but once you have been at your job for a while, you should be able to do that for yourself.

LEARNING TO DELEGATE

Do you have office help? Does it sometimes seem to be more of a hindrance than a help? Almost everyone can use a lesson or two in learning how to delegate. Here are some pointers.

Begin by giving good directions. It's surprisingly hard to give an assistant clear, cogent directions. It is always worth the effort, however. If you skip steps, you run the risk of having the task done badly, which reflects badly on you. Worse, you may find yourself giving up your own time to redo the work of others. Think the task through before you give oral or written directions. Ask yourself:

1. What materials will the worker need?
2. What must he or she do first? second? third?
3. How much time should be spent on the task?
4. How will the worker know if the task has been done correctly?

Use your answers to these questions to explain the task to others.

Assess the work of others and adjust your expectations accordingly. Don't let things get out of hand; check on a new assistant's work as often as you need to for the first few weeks. If the assistant is capable, give her or him more responsibility. If certain tasks are consistently troublesome, reassign the work to others and find something else for your assistant to do. Of course, if your new helper cannot do the work, you must alert your supervisor. Don't allow your time to be taken over by the errors and flaws of a worker who just isn't working out.

Don't do it all yourself. It's tempting to say, "I can do it better, so I might as well do it." Your goal should be to train your assistant over time to do the task as well as you would. You may sacrifice some quality at first, but you'll make it up in the time you save for essential tasks of your own.

CREATIVE PROBLEM SOLVING

Time-management problems often call for creative solutions. Let's take a look at some typical situations: Worker X is constantly bothered by phone calls as he is trying to record payments and organize bills. Worker Y is called upon to take the minutes for every meeting in her department, so she never seems to finish her own correspondence. Worker Z simply cannot juggle all the tasks he has to do—a seemingly infinite amount of filing, record keeping, and word processing keeps him working long after 5 p.m. every day.

The steps to solving the above problems can also be applied to your own office work.

Identify the cause. In Worker X's case, he handles all initial contacts from people calling the office during the business day. Worker Y is constantly interrupted by meetings. Worker Z has too much paperwork.

Suggest an alternative. Worker X could set aside one time of day for uninterrupted work on the billing system, perhaps taking an early lunch and working during lunch hour, when most calls are handled through the receptionist. Worker Y might ask that other staff members take turns taking minutes, thereby freeing her to do her more essential work. Worker Z might ask for a temporary assistant, using a time-management chart (Figure 3.1) to plead his case with management.

Test and evaluate your solution. Try your alternative for a week or two. How do you like it? How do your co-workers like it? Does it truly eliminate your time-management problem, or would a different alternative be better?

A PLACE FOR EVERYTHING

Time-and-motion studies proved one thing: People work faster when they move around less. You will move around less in your office if you have an orderly place for everything.

Astonishing amounts of time can be wasted searching for

misfiled memos, misplaced invoices, or even lost pencils in a messy desk drawer. The better you organize your physical space, the more likely your time will be spent doing the things you were hired to do. (See Figure 1.1 for some tips on this subject.)

DEADLINE PRESSURE

Certain offices face constant deadline pressure. Employees who work in magazine publishing may have one day a week or one week a month when deadline pressures hit. Employees in manufacturing may rush to fill orders at certain times of the month and slow down in between. A new employee soon learns to adjust his or her schedule accordingly.

If your work requires deadlines, you can benefit from using a work-flow calendar that tracks your work and notes when each part of the job must be finished. Fill it in by working backward, from the deadline to the present time. The following sample illustrates the work involved in meeting a publishing deadline:

Work-Flow Calendar

M		T		W		TH		F
7	←	8	←	9	←	10	←	11
copywrite		copywrite		copywrite		get approval		rewrite
14	←	15	←	16	←	17	←	18
input		input		layout		edit		edit
21	←	22	←	23	←	24	←	25
work to printer				proofread galleys		pick up finished work		DEADLINE

Fig. 3.3

SEASONAL PRESSURE

Seasonal pressure is a particular kind of deadline pressure. Employees of Florida hotels may be frantically busy in winter and able to relax as the spring break ends. Employees of accounting firms may work long hours and weekends from January through April 15, income tax day. Some employees of universities may be active all during the school year and relatively idle from graduation until just before fall registration.

If your company is affected by seasonal pressure, it will affect your lifestyle. Chances are, you will take your vacations in slow periods and work overtime in season. This can work out nicely if your hobbies and pastimes correspond to the free time you gain thanks to seasonal deadlines.

HOMEWORK

You may be employed for fifty years and never need to take work home. On the other hand, most of us end up taking work home at least occasionally. If you find yourself with more homework than you would like, ask yourself:

1. Am I working efficiently during office hours? If not, how could I improve my efficiency?
2. Am I given more work than I can realistically handle during regular hours? If so, can I ask for help?
3. Is everyone else taking work home, or am I the only one? Am I taking work home just because I think it's expected?
4. Am I taking work home only when a deadline is approaching, or is there a constant overflow of work?
5. Do I actually work better at home? Does my employer allow employees to work certain hours at home and others at the office?

If you work at home occasionally, make sure you have your on private space in which to operate. A desk or table with a good lamp and small bookshelf tucked in a quiet corner will do. Distance yourself from distractions for maximum efficiency.

4

Handling Grievances

- Title VII
- Americans with Disabilities Act
- Age Discrimination in Employment Act
- Equal Pay Act
- Sexual Harassment
- Working within Your Company
- Working within a Union
- Working within the Legal System

"A fair day's wages for a fair day's work"—Thomas Carlyle called this "the everlasting right of man." Today, we might call it "the everlasting right of humankind," but our essential meaning would be the same: If we work fairly, we should be fairly rewarded. For many of us, this is in fact the case. Some of us, however, face obstacles to that fundamental right. Intolerance, insensitivity, discrimination, and unfair labor practices cause some of us to be mistreated, harassed, illegally dismissed, or undercompensated. Should you ever find yourself in such a situation, this chapter will give you some basic information about your rights and recourses.

TITLE VII

The Civil Rights Act of 1964 contains within it a section known as Title VII, which forbids discrimination in employment based on race, color, religion, sex, or national origin. Any employer with 15 or more employees must abide by this law. Among other areas of employment, the law covers discrimination in recruitment and hiring, promotion and transfer, and compensation and benefits. Title VII also established an agency, the Equal Employment Opportunity Commission (EEOC), to enforce the law and protect the nation's workers. The law allows certain state agencies to share the burden of enforcement with this federal agency.

AMERICANS WITH DISABILITIES ACT

This 1990 law not only prohibits discrimination in hiring and other employment terms, but it also requires employers to provide "reasonable accommodation" for workers with disabilities. Job listings must include all required physical and intellectual skills for the job. An office itself may have to be altered to conform to the worker's job-related needs. For example, Braille elevator buttons might be installed for a blind worker, or a special desk might be purchased for a worker in a wheelchair. This law affects all businesses with more than 15 employees, but "reasonable accommodation" has a certain amount of flexibility—a very small business is not expected to go into bankruptcy in order to accommodate a single worker.

AGE DISCRIMINATION IN EMPLOYMENT ACT

This law, first passed in 1967, is designed to protect workers over the age of 40 who work for companies that employ 20 or more workers. It covers age-based discrimination in hiring, compensation, and so on. This kind of discrimination is sometimes difficult to prove unless it is widespread within a company. Some states have additional laws that also protect younger workers. Compliance with the law may be waived for jobs with special physical requirements—firefighters and airline pilots, for example, may legally be required to retire at a certain age.

EQUAL PAY ACT

In any business having two or more employees, workers must receive equal pay and equal benefits for equal work. The exception is for pay based on seniority or productivity. This 1963 law was developed to avoid a certain kind of sex discrimination in a system that historically paid women less than men. How do you define "equal work"? If you have two office assistants—one male and one female—hired at the same time, both should receive the same salary. But, if you are one out of three female office assistants, you have to compare your compensation to that of a man whose employment at your company requires responsibility equivalent to your own. Use common sense to assess comparable worth. A bookkeeper may work under circumstances similar to yours; a lawyer probably does not.

SEXUAL HARASSMENT

This is the EEOC's legal definition of sexual harassment. Unwelcome sexual advances, requests for sexual favors, and other verbal or physical conduct of a sexual nature constitute sexual harassment when:

1. submission to such conduct is made either explicitly or implicitly a term or condition of an individual's employment,

2. submission to or rejection of such conduct by an individual is used as the basis for employment decisions affecting such individual, or
3. such conduct has the purpose or effect of interfering with an individual's work performance or creating an intimidating, hostile or offensive work environment.

Sexual harassment is illegal under Title VII, which provides assistance for workers in companies with 15 or more employees. Employers are legally accountable for harassment by their employees against each other, but it may be up to the harassed worker to bring the harassment to the employer's attention.

WORKING WITHIN YOUR COMPANY

The ideal way to handle a grievance is to deal directly with the person responsible, ask for satisfaction, and receive it. In cases of sexual harassment, a strong, negative reaction may be all that is needed to stop the harasser. Many companies have specific guidelines and policies outlined in a handbook, and specific ways of handling any breaches of those guidelines. You can often prepare your own case by using the company's own rules and regulations to demonstrate its failures. Here is an example of the way an in-company complaint might be prepared and presented.

Preparing and Presenting a Grievance

1. *Prepare your evidence.* In any case of alleged discrimination, your weapons are your work records or appraisals, your company's written policy, facts and figures you yourself have gathered, and the law. The more factual and less emotional your initial presentation is, the more likely you will be to make your point.
2. *Decide what it is you want.* Do you want to be reinstated, to receive back pay, to work in safety, to establish a new company policy? Decide on your goals before moving forward with your complaint.
3. *Determine where to bring the evidence.* Your first step should be to work within the office hierarchy. See your immediate supervisor, unless he or she is the problem. Your company may handle grievances through the human resources department or through a special grievance committee. There may be an ombudsperson whose job it is to handle such cases.
4. *Present your case coolly and accurately.* If your company is in violation of Title VII or another law, have the relevant passages ready to read. Use your work records to show that your mistreatment is not the result of poor performance. Present any relevant data you have found—dates of harassment, ages of employees, pay scales of equivalent jobs—whatever makes your particular case stronger. Then tell what you expect to receive should your complaint be found valid.

Fig. 4.1

A large company may have a formal procedure to investigate your claims of discrimination; if you work for a small company, you may simply have a conversation with your supervisor. In either case, you should be given a time frame in which your complaint will be reviewed and assessed. If you do not receive a response within that time, follow up.

WORKING WITHIN A UNION

If you belong to a union, you probably have a standard operating procedure to follow in case of a grievance. You may take your complaint to your shop representative, who will compare your account to your union's collective bargaining agreement to see whether any terms have been violated. If the union decides to proceed, the union itself will probably file a grievance on your behalf. If you need to appear before your company's grievance committee, a union representative may accompany you.

At any rate, the rules in Figure 4.1 for preparation of grievances apply to you, too. It is best to be armed with evidence and figures before you visit your union leadership.

WORKING WITHIN THE LEGAL SYSTEM

There are times when the best prepared, most clear-cut discrimination case fails to win over management. If your grievance is ignored, laughed off, treated with contempt—or worse, with threats of dismissal—you may decide to take legal action.

Understand that this is a big step. Very few discrimination cases go on to win multimillion dollar settlements. Most take some time to settle. Only you can determine whether this is the right step for you.

The agency that handles discrimination and harassment lawsuits is the EEOC. There are branches throughout the United States; to find the one nearest you, call 1-(800)-USA-EEOC.

In many cases, the EEOC requires that the incident or incidents described in the grievance have occurred within the last 180 days. You may file your grievance in person at one of the ranch offices or in writing. The statement you file must contain ames and details of the alleged discrimination. The sugges-ions in Figure 4.1 can help you here. Note that only about one ercent of EEOC grievances ever go to trial. Assuming that it nds your grievance valid, the agency has 180 days to try to ne-otiate a settlement with your employer. If no settlement is eached, the agency may either bring suit on your behalf, or ive you what is called a "right-to-sue" notice, encouraging you o file a lawsuit on your own if you choose to do so.

Alternatively, you may file a claim with a state agency. Al-bama, Arkansas, and Virginia are the only states without a Fair mployment Practices law on the books. Other states have gencies, usually human rights commissions or departments of abor, that will take on discrimination cases if they find reason-ble cause. In some cases, the state laws differ from the federal aws described above; ask the agency to explain the laws as ney apply to your case.

If you win a court case, you may expect to obtain any of sev-ral possible awards.

Possible Awards in Discrimination Cases

Injunctions	The court may order your employer to cease all discriminatory practices.
Back Pay	You may receive any salary you lost due to unfair dismissal, forced retirement, or unjust demotion.
Reinstatement	The court may order your employer to give you your job back, with benefits and seniority restored.
Hiring	If the court finds that you were not hired due to discrimination, it can order the company to hire you.
Fees and Costs	Your employer may be required to pick up part of the legal costs of filing your suit.
Compensatory Damages	A limited amount of money may be awarded to compensate you for personal injury such as stress. There are caps on such awards for victims of discrimination based on sex, religion, or disability.
Punitive Damages	This monetary award has the same limits as compensatory damages. You may receive such an award if the discrimination you reported is found to be intentional and malicious.

Fig. 4.2

Be aware that many state agencies have no power to assess punitive or compensatory damages.

II

Communicating in Writing

5

Grammar and Usage

- Parts of Speech
- Types of Sentences
- Phrases and Clauses
- Subject-Verb Agreement
- Pronoun-Antecedent Agreement
- Correcting Pronoun Errors
- Correcting Verb Errors
- Correcting Adjective and Adverb Errors
- Correcting Phrase and Clause Errors
- Correcting Sentence Errors
- Frequently Misused Words

Your job, whatever industry you work in, involves communication. Possessing good written communication skills will help you do your job more effectively. Understanding and using the rules of standard written English will provide the basis for building these skills. This chapter reviews those rules, focusing particularly on correcting common errors.

PARTS OF SPEECH

Nouns

• A **noun** names a person, place, thing, or idea. Nouns come in two classes, **common** and **proper.**

Proper nouns name specific people, places, or things, and they always begin with a capital letter.

Common nouns name unspecified people, places, things, or ideas. Some nouns, called **compound nouns,** contain more than one word.

Nouns

	Person	Place	Thing	Idea
Common	woman	city	computer	hope
Proper	Lydia	Chicago	Macintosh	

Compound Nouns

Common	vice president	skyscraper	word processor
Proper	Mrs. Ruiz	Sears Tower	Epson Equity II

Fig. 5.1

Pronouns

• A **pronoun** is used in place of a noun or nouns. You are very familiar with **personal pronouns;** you use them every day.

Personal Pronouns

	Singular		Plural	
First Person	I, me	my, mine	we, us	our, ours
Second Person	you	your, yours	you	your, yours
Third Person	he, him	his	they, them	their, theirs
	she, her	her, hers		
	it	its		

Fig. 5.2

Reflexive pronouns are forms of personal pronouns used to *reflect* back on the subject being discussed.

I did the job *myself.*
You did the job *yourself.*
He did the job *himself.*
She did the job *herself.*
It did the job *itself.*
We did the job *ourselves.*
You did the job *yourselves.*
They did the job *themselves.*

Demonstrative pronouns refer to specific people, places, things, or ideas.

***This* is a great plan.**
***That* is a great plan.**
***These* are great plans.**
***Those* are great plans.**

Indefinite pronouns, as their name suggests, refer to unspecified people, places, things, or ideas.

***All* approved the agenda.**
***Both* approved the agenda.**
***Few* approved the agenda.**
***Someone* approved the agenda.**

Relative pronouns act to *relate* a clause to the subject of the sentence. These words are relative pronouns:

that which who whoever whom whomever whose

Interrogative pronouns begin interrogative sentences.

***Who* chaired the council?** ***Whose* was the first motion?**
***What* was decided?** ***Whom* shall I inform?**

Verbs

• A **verb** expresses an action or links words in a sentence. **Action verbs** are either *transitive* or *intransitive*.

Transitive verbs have objects that receive the action.

I sent the memo. **Jack repaired the machine.**

Intransitive verbs have no object.

The memo *ended* abruptly. **The copying machine *exploded.***

Linking verbs may be thought of as expressing a state of being rather than an action.

She *is* a good boss. **The temp *seems* competent.**
This coffee *smells* awful. **We *became* increasingly worried.**

Most linking verbs are forms of the irregular verb *to be*.

Verbs are the words in a sentence that express time. They tell whether the idea being communicated happened in the past, is happening in the present, or will happen in the future. All verbs have six **tenses,** which are formed from the **principal parts** of the verb. Here is an example of a regular verb with its six tenses.

Six Tenses of a Regular Verb		
	First Person	**Third Person**
Present	I ask	she asks
Past	I asked	she asked
Future	I will/shall ask	she will ask
Present Perfect	I have asked	she has asked
Past Perfect	I had asked	she had asked
Future Perfect	I will have asked	she will have asked

Fig. 5.3

Adjectives

• An **adjective** modifies a noun or pronoun. It makes the noun or pronoun more specific by telling about its size, color, type, number, and so on. Watch how the use of adjectives can transform a simple sentence and how using precise adjectives can change a sentence's meaning.

Give me those files.

size	**Give me those *bulky* files.**
color	**Give me those *red* files.**
type	**Give me those *legal* files.**
number	**Give me those *five* files.**

Certain words you have met before as *demonstrative pronouns* may be used as adjectives when they modify a noun or another pronoun. In the sentences above, *those* is such a word.

Adjectives may precede a noun or pronoun, as in the examples above, or they may follow a *linking verb* or otherwise be divided from the word they modify.

The files on the shelf were *red*.

***Red* in color, the files sat on the shelf.**

Articles are special adjectives. *The* is a **definite article;** it refers to a specific person, place, thing, or idea, which may be singular or plural.

***The* taxis have arrived.** **Did you call *the* electrician?**

A and *an* are **indefinite articles**; they refer to unspecified people, places, things, or ideas, all of which must be singular.

***A* taxi has arrived.** **Did you call *an* electrician?**

Adverbs

- An **adverb** modifies a verb, adjective, or adverb. It makes the word being modified more specific by telling where, when, how, how long, how much, or to what extent. Like adjectives, adverbs can transform a simple sentence and change its meaning. In these cases, the adverb modifies the verb *give.*

Give me those files.

where	**Give me *back* those files.**
when	***Now* give me those files.**
how	**Give me those files *carefully*.**

Adverbs that modify adjectives usually tell how much or to what extent.

modifying an adjective	**That was an *unusually* long seminar.**
modifying an adverb	**The speaker spoke *quite* brilliantly.**

Prepositions

• A **preposition** shows the relationship between a noun or pronoun and another word in a sentence. Prepositions can greatly alter the meaning of your sentence.

He wrote to the President. **He wrote with the President.**
He wrote about the President. **He wrote for the President.**

Common Prepositions

about	above	across	after	against	along
around	at	before	behind	below	beside
between	by	during	for	from	in
into	like	near	of	on	onto
out	over	per	since	through	to
under	until	upon	with	within	without

Fig. 5.4

Conjunctions

• A **conjunction** joins words, phrases, or clauses. Conjunctions come in three varieties.

Coordinating conjunctions connect like words or ideas. The most common coordinating conjunctions are *and, but,* and *or.* These conjunctions make specific connections having to do with addition, contrast, or choice.

addition	**The law library is dark *and* dusty.**
contrast	**The clerk is tired, *but* she has hours of work left.**
choice	**Leave the book on the desk *or* near the bookcart.**

Other coordinating conjunctions include *for, so, yet,* and *whereas.*

Correlative conjunctions are paired conjunctions that connect like words or ideas.

The law library is *both* dark *and* dusty.
The clerk is not *only* tired, but *also* she has the flu.
***Either* leave the book on the desk *or* check it out.**

Other correlative conjunctions include *neither/nor, just as/so,* and *whether/or.*

Subordinating conjunctions introduce dependent clauses (see below).

Common Subordinating Conjunctions

after	although	as	as if	because	before
if	since	than	though	unless	until
when	whenever	where	whereas	wherever	while

Fig. 5.5

Interjections

• An **interjection** expresses strong feeling. An interjection is separated from the rest of the sentence by a comma or an exclamation point.

Wow! **That was an exciting report!**
Well, **I did not understand it.**
It was as clear as day! My goodness!

TYPES OF SENTENCES

A **sentence** is a group of words that express a complete thought. There are four basic sentence types.

Declarative sentences tell or state.

We ordered fifty units. **The laptop computer is useful.**

Interrogative sentences ask.

What did we order? **Is the laptop computer useful?**

Imperative sentences command or request.

Order fifty units. **Please try the laptop computer.**

Exclamatory sentences exclaim.

What a huge order this is! **Wow, the laptop computer is terrific!**

Every sentence has a **subject** and **predicate**. The **subject** is the part of the sentence about which something is being said. The **predicate** is the part of the sentence that contains the verb and says something about the subject.

My supervisor	**WORKS HARD.**	***Her job***	**SEEMS UNENDING.**
subject	**predicate**	**subject**	**predicate**

The subject of an imperative sentence is understood to be *you,* even though it is not stated.

(*You*) ORDER FIFTY UNITS.

Compound sentences contain more than one subject and predicate. The two parts of a compound sentence are usually joined by a conjunction.

> ***My supervisor*** **WORKS HARD, but** ***her job*** **SEEMS UNENDING.**

PHRASES AND CLAUSES

Phrases

• A **phrase** is a group of related words. A phrase is part of a sentence, but it does not contain its own subject and predicate. Phrases come in several types, but they are always used either as nouns or as modifiers.

Gerund phrases are used as nouns in a sentence. A gerund phrase contains a *gerund*, the *-ing* form of a verb used as a noun.

> ***Understanding the new word processing program*** **will be a challenge.**

Infinitive phrases may be used as nouns or as modifiers. An infinitive phrase contains an **infinitive**, the form of a verb that includes the word *to*.

as a noun	***To complete this task*** **will take some time.**
as an adjective	**He is the right person** ***to ask for help.***
as an adverb	**I am always happy** ***to meet another Texan.***

Participial phrases are used as adjectives. A participial phrase contains a **participle,** an *-ing* or *-ed* form of a verb used as an adjective.

Looking somewhat smug, **he announced his plan.**

We later saw him *dressed in a three-piece suit.*

Prepositional phrases are used as adjectives or adverbs. A prepositional phrase begins with a preposition and ends with a noun or a pronoun.

as an adjective	**The office *next to mine* is noisy.**
as an adverb	**Please sit *in that chair.***

Clauses

• A **clause** is a group of related words that contains its own subject and predicate. Like phrases, clauses are parts of sentences. There are two main kinds of clauses.

Dependent clauses cannot stand alone. Although a dependent clause contains both subject and predicate, it does not express a complete thought. Dependent clauses are often called **subordinate clauses.** Each clause begins with a **subordinating conjunction.**

After you finish, **see Mrs. Johnson.**
She will not help us *unless we ask.*

Independent clauses can stand alone as sentences. Two independent clauses may be put together to form a **compound sentence,** or an independent clause and a dependent clause may be put together to form a **complex sentence.**

compound	***We asked a question,*** **but** ***the speaker ignored us.***
complex	***We asked a question*** **because we had some concerns.**

SUBJECT-VERB AGREEMENT

Nouns and pronouns are either **singular**—referring to one person, place, thing, or idea—or they are **plural**, referring to more than one. Like nouns and pronouns, verbs refer to number. In a sentence, a singular subject must be paired with a singular verb, and a plural subject must be paired with a plural verb. In the present tense, the singular form of most verbs ends in *-s* or *-es*. This can be confusing, since the *plural* form of most nouns also ends in *-s* or *-es*.

singular subject and verb	***A notebook*** **CONTAINS** ***my records.***
plural subject and verb	***Notebooks*** **CONTAIN** ***my records.***

It does not matter whether words come between the subject and verb or whether subject and verb are in reversed order—the subject and verb must still agree.

A notebook **covered with scribbles CONTAINS my records.**
Notebooks **in my file cabinet CONTAIN my records.**
DOES that ***notebook*** **CONTAIN your records?**
Do those ***notebooks*** **CONTAIN your records?**

Some nouns can be either singular or plural. These **collective nouns** name single groups, and can act as singular subjects. However, when the individual members of the group act separately, the nouns can be used as plural subjects.

singular	**The** ***committee*** **sponsors the bill.**
plural	**The** ***committee*** **suggest several amendments.**

Other collective nouns you may need to use include *audience, class, faculty, group, team, union,* and *workforce.*

Indefinite pronouns can be tricky. Most are singular, some are plural, and others can be either, just as collective nouns can.

Indefinite Pronouns

Singular	another	each	anybody/anyone/anything		
	either	much	everybody/everyone/everything		
	neither	one	nobody/no one/nothing		
			somebody/someone/something		
Plural	both	few	many	several	
Either	all	any	most	none	some

Fig. 5.6

Whether an indefinite pronoun such as *some* is singular or plural depends on the phrase it introduces.

singular ***Some*** **of our product TRAVELS overseas.**

plural ***Some*** **of our employees WORK overtime.**

Subjects joined by *and* are paired with a plural verb. Subjects joined by *or* or *nor* are paired with a verb that agrees with the subject nearest that verb.

Mr. Crawford **and his** ***assistant*** **RUN that division.**
Mr. Crawford **or his** ***assistant*** **RUNS that division.**
Mr. Crawford **or his** ***assistants*** **RUN that division.**

Certain subjects appear plural but nevertheless require singular verbs.

Fifty dollars **SEEMS a lot to pay.**
Economics **GIVES us the best long-term view.**

On the other hand, some subjects look singular but always take plural verbs.

The *data* CONTRADICT what he is saying.
***Bacteria* REPRODUCE very rapidly.**

PRONOUN-ANTECEDENT AGREEMENT

Like nouns, pronouns are singular or plural. In addition, pronouns are masculine, feminine, or neuter—they have *gender* as well as *number.* Remember, a pronoun replaces a noun or nouns in a sentence. The words it replaces are the pronoun's *antecedent.*

Employees may refer to *their* handbooks for information.

That rule is confusing; *it* may be misunderstood.

Jane and I think that *we* should rewrite the handbook.

CORRECTING PRONOUN ERRORS

ERROR 1: Your pronoun and antecedent do not agree.

This can happen if you do not really understand the structure of your sentence, if you forget whether an indefinite pronoun is singular or plural, or if you try unsuccessfully to make a sentence non-sexist without rewriting it.

incorrect	**Mark and Diego ordered his furniture.**
correct	**Mark and Diego ordered *their* furniture.**
incorrect	**Each of the women took their vacation.**

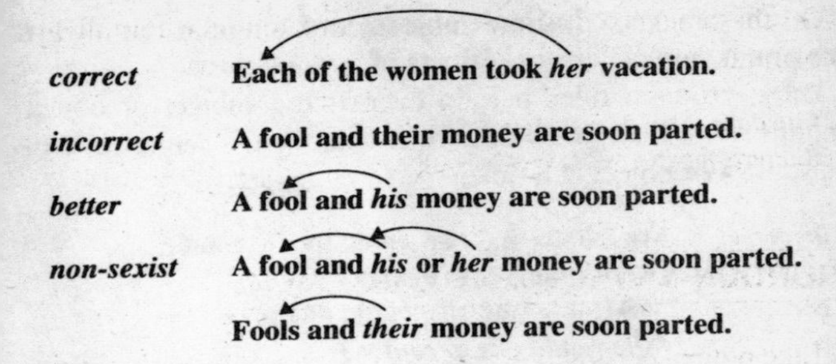

ERROR 2: You use subject and object pronouns incorrectly.

Besides having *number* and *gender,* pronouns have **case.** The case of a pronoun depends on how it is used in a sentence.

Subject and Object Pronouns

	Singular		**Plural**	
	Subject	***Object***	***Subject***	***Object***
First Person	I	me	we	us
Second Person	you	you	you	you
Third Person	he	him	they	them
	she	her		
	it	it		

Fig. 5.7

A pronoun used in the subject of a sentence will always be a **subject pronoun.** A pronoun that follows a linking verb and refers back to the subject will also be a subject pronoun:

incorrect	**This is her.**
correct	**This is *she*.**

Object pronouns may be used as **direct objects** that receive the action of a verb, **indirect objects** that tell to whom or for whom an action occurs, or **objects of prepositions.**

These pronoun rules pertain even if the subject or object contains more than one word. To check, try the sentence with one subject or object at a time.

incorrect	**Mr. Dobbs and her would like to confer.**
	[Her would like to confer.]
correct	**Mr. Dobbs and *she* would like to confer.**
	[She would like to confer.]
incorrect	**Please have Ms. Byars call Mr. Dobbs and I.**
	[Please have Ms. Byars call I.]
correct	**Please have Ms. Byars call Mr. Dobbs and *me.***
	[Please have Ms. Byars call me.]

The same rules apply to *who,* which is a subject pronoun, and *whom,* which is an object pronoun. You must decide how the word is being used in the sentence and choose the case accordingly. When in doubt, try substituting *he* or *him* in the sentence.

as a subject	**Who is on the phone?**
	[He is on the phone.]
as a direct object	**Whom did you call?**
	[You did call him.]
as the object of a preposition	**By whom was the message delivered?**
	[The message was delivered by him.]

ERROR 3: You use nonexistent reflexive pronouns.

incorrect	**He gave hisself a pat on the back.**
correct	**He gave *himself* a pat on the back.**

(See page 51 for a list of reflexive pronouns.)

ERROR 4: *You name yourself first.*

This is often an error in spoken English, but it is especially glaring in written English. It's an easy rule to remember—just be polite, and let others go first.

incorrect	**I and he went to the coffee shop.**
correct	***He and I* went to the coffee shop.**
incorrect	**Please order lunch for me and Ms. Lopez.**
correct	**Please order lunch for *Ms. Lopez and me.***

CORRECTING VERB ERRORS

ERROR 1: *You mix up tenses.*

In general, you should choose one of the six tenses (see Figure 5.3) and stick to it.

incorrect	**I am talking, and he told me to sit down.**
correct	**I *was* talking, and he told me to sit down.**

ERROR 2: *You use the passive voice too much.*

In the active voice, the subject acts. In the passive voice, the subject receives the action.

incorrect	**Passive voice is used by you.**
correct	**You use active voice.**

The active voice is livelier, and usually clearer.

ERROR 3: *You misuse irregular verb forms.*

We will tackle some of these errors under "Frequently Misused Words" (p. 72). In any language, irregular verb forms must simply be memorized. Some verb forms are related to each other, but no one rule covers them all. Here are a few especially useful verbs whose forms you should know, arranged by type.

Common Irregular Verb Forms

Present	Past	Present/Past/ Future Perfect
[be] am, is, are	was, were	been
do	did	done
go	went	gone
have	had	had
draw	drew	drawn
fly	flew	flown
grow	grew	grown
know	knew	known
eat	ate	eaten
break	broke	broken
choose	chose	chosen
freeze	froze	frozen
speak	spoke	spoken
buy	bought	bought
catch	caught	caught
fight	fought	fought
drink	drank	drunk
sing	sang	sung
sink	sank	sunk
swim	swam	swum
come	came	come
run	ran	run
cost	cost	cost
put	put	put
quit	quit	quit

Fig. 5.8

ERROR 4: You use nonstandard verb forms.

Nonstandard English has its place, but your job will usually require you to follow standard rules.

incorrect	**She be a good technician.**
correct	**She *is* a good technician.**

CORRECTING ADJECTIVE AND ADVERB ERRORS

ERROR 1: You use nonstandard forms of modifiers.

incorrect	**My program ran most quickest of all.**
correct	**My program ran *quickest* of all.**
incorrect	**That model is usefuller than this one.**
correct	**That model is *more useful* than this one.**

Adjectives and adverbs may be used to compare the objects or actions they modify. Most one-syllable modifiers add *-er* or *-est* when they are used this way. Longer modifiers add the word *more* or *most.* Here are some examples.

comparing two things	**nicer**	**more cordial**
comparing more than two things	**nicest**	**most cordial**
comparing two actions	**harder**	**more difficult**
comparing more than two actions	**hardest**	**most difficult**

ERROR 2: You misuse irregular comparative and superlative forms.

There are a few adjectives and adverbs that break the rules. As with irregular verbs, these forms must be memorized.

Common Irregular Modifiers

Modifier	Comparative Form	Superlative Form
bad	worse	worst
good	better	best
well	better	best
many	more	most
much	more	most

Fig. 5.9

ERROR 3: You use double negatives.

A sentence may contain no more than one negative adverb. Rewrite sentences that contain more than one, replacing one of the negatives with a positive form.

Negative and Positive Adverbs

hardly/almost	never/ever
no/any	nobody/anybody
none/any	no one/anyone
nothing/anything	nowhere/ anywhere

Fig. 5.10

incorrect	**I didn't hear nothing about the meeting.**
correct	**I didn't hear *anything* about the meeting.**
	I heard nothing about the meeting.
incorrect	**We never saw no brochure about it.**
correct	**We never saw *any* brochure about it.**
	We saw no brochure about it.

CORRECTING PHRASE AND CLAUSE ERRORS

ERROR 1: You split infinitives.

An *infinitive phrase* (see page 58), contains the form of a verb that includes the word *to.* Try not to insert any words between *to* and the verb in this construction. Be careful: *to* may be used as a preposition rather than as part of a verb. This rule *only* applies to infinitives.

incorrect **We need to carefully move the computer.**
correct **We need to move the computer carefully.**

ERROR 2: You dangle participles.

You may have heard of **dangling participles**; you may even have dangled a few. Now you'll see how to avoid doing so. A participle is a verb form; it is often used to begin a **participial phrase** (see page 58). When the participial phrase does not have anything in the sentence to modify, we say that it is left "dangling." Often, this makes for a confusing sentence.

incorrect **Walking into the hall, my seat was already taken.**
[Who's walking—my seat?]
correct **Walking into the hall, I saw that my seat was already taken.**
incorrect **Posted on the bulletin board, we were surprised.**
[Are we posted on the board?]
correct **Posted on the bulletin board, the notice surprised us.**

ERROR 3: You misplace modifiers.

This is a very common error that is similar to Error 2 above. A phrase or clause must be placed as close to the word it modifies as possible. Otherwise, the meaning of the sentence can be muddled.

incorrect **I enjoyed meeting new people in Seattle at the convention.**
[Are you meeting people who are new to Seattle?]

correct **At the convention in Seattle, I enjoyed meeting new people.**

incorrect **The chairs were ordered by the manager for the conference room.**
[Does the manager manage the conference room?]

correct **The manager ordered the chairs for the conference room.**

incorrect **My lunch is on the table which I never got to eat.**
[You never got to eat the table?]

correct **My lunch, which I never got to eat, is on the table.**

CORRECTING SENTENCE ERRORS

ERROR 1: Your sentences are incomplete.

A sentence must contain a subject and predicate and state a complete thought. A subject alone, a predicate alone, a dependent clause, or part of a compound sentence beginning with a conjunction does not equal a sentence. Such partial sentences are called **sentence fragments**. Extreme length and appropriate punctuation cannot transform a fragment into a sentence.

fragment **Her newly won, hard-fought contract.**
[needs a predicate]

fragment	**Never received a better offer.** ***[needs a subject]***
fragment	**Because it seemed like a good idea at the time.** ***[needs an independent clause]***
sentence	**I agree.** ***[contains both a subject and a predicate, and expresses a complex thought]***

ERROR 2: Your sentences run on.

Run-on sentences are compound, complex, or compound-complex (containing at least two independent clauses plus a dependent clause). It is possible to add clauses and punctuation to a sentence until it extends for pages, but it is not advisable. Remember, a sentence's purpose is to express a thought. The longer a sentence is, the more likely you are to lose track of that thought. You can usually chop a run-on sentence into two or more sentences and improve your communication in the process.

run-on	**Because we needed accounting help, I called the human resources manager, Mrs. Chan, and I told her our problem, and she suggested that I call the firm of Basker and Chase; they have helped in the past.**
better	**Because we needed accounting help, I called the human resources manager, Mrs. Chan. I told her our problem, and she suggested that I call the firm of Basker and Chase. They have helped in the past.**

ERROR 3: Your sentences are choppy and dull.

Try to vary your sentences to add interest to your writing. Review a piece of writing you have recently completed. Do many of the sentences begin with the same word? Could you combine any sentences to vary the sentence length? (See page 58 for examples of compound sentences.) Could you use different types of sentences? (See page 57 for examples of sentence types.) Variety adds spice to writing as well as to life.

FREQUENTLY MISUSED WORDS

A/AN	Use **a** before a consonant sound. Use **an** before a vowel sound. I read **a** history of a union. In about **an** hour, the author will address **an** audience.
ACCEPT/EXCEPT	**Accept** means "receive" or "agree to." He will happily *accept* the award. **Except** means "but" or "excluding." Everyone voted *except* Ms. Rivers.
ADVICE/ADVISE	**Advice** is a noun; **advise** is a verb. Nobody listened to my *advice*. I was hired to *advise* the committee.
AFFECT/EFFECT	**Affect** is a verb meaning "change." **Effect** can be a verb meaning cause," or it can be a noun meaning "result." How will the storm *affect* our plans? It will *effect* a change in dates. Rescheduling will be the main *effect*.
ALL TOGETHER/ ALTOGETHER	**All together** means "as one." **Altogether** means "absolutely." Let's repeat the oath *all together*. That sounded *altogether* awful.
AMONG/BETWEEN	**Among** refers to three or more things.

Between refers to two things.
It was passed *between* Ed and Bev.
It was passed *among* the five members.

A WHILE/AWHILE

If the word is an adverb, use **awhile**. If it is the object of a preposition, use **a while**.
Let's think about this *awhile*.
Let's think about this for *a while*.

BESIDE/BESIDES

Beside means "next to."
Besides means "in addition" or "furthermore."
Sit down *beside* the potted palm.
Besides the palm, what plants do you own?
I don't like plants; *besides*, I have allergies.

BRING/TAKE

Bring refers to coming toward; **take** refers to going away.
Please *bring* me that file.
Now *take* the file to Ms. Kyawa.

CONTINUAL/
CONTINUOUS

Continual means "recurring at frequent intervals."
Continuous means "unceasing."
False alarms were a *continual* interruption.
The alarm made a *continuous* howl.

DIFFERENT FROM/
DIFFERENT THAN

Never use *different than* except when *than* is a subordinating conjunction introducing a dependent clause.
He is *different from* my former boss.
He is *different than* I thought he'd be.

FARTHER/FURTHER

Farther refers to distance; **further** refers to extent.
Houston is *farther* than we planned to go.
We have *further* concerns about the trip.

FEWER/LESS

Fewer refers to "how many"; **less** refers to "how much." Use *fewer* with plural nouns and *less* with singular nouns.
There were *fewer* orders this month than last.
As a result, we made *less* money.

GOOD/WELL

Good is an adjective; use it before a noun or after a linking verb.
Well can be an adjective meaning "healthy." Most often, however, it is an adverb.
It was a *good* test of our skills.
Are you feeling *well*?
We did *well* on the test.

HAVE/OF

Have is part of a verb; **of** is a preposition.
She could *have* been more polite.
The visitor must *have* felt insulted.
I was ashamed *of* her.

HOPEFUL/
HOPEFULLY

Hopeful is an adjective meaning "full of hope."
Hopefully is an adverb meaning "in a hopeful way"—*not* "let us hope."
We are *hopeful* that this product will sell.
We applied *hopefully* to the patent office.

IN TO/INTO

In to is an adverb followed by a preposition; **into** is a preposition referring to entry.
Management gave *in to* the union's demands.
The truck pulled *in to* the loading dock.
Our ballots went *into* the box.
Load the boxes *into* the truck.

LAY/LIE

Lay is a transitive verb (see page 52) meaning "to place."
Lie is an intransitive verb (see page 52) meaning "to recline."

Lay and Lie

Present	Past	Present/Past/Future Perfect
lay	laid	laid
lie	lay	lain

Fig. 5.11

Please *lay* the papers on the desk.
You may *lie* down in the nurse's office.

LEARN/TEACH

Learn means "receive knowledge."
Teach means "impart knowledge."
The student interns *learn* quickly.
Teach them to use the fax modem.

LEAVE/LET

Leave implies "departure."
Let implies "permission."
Leave her alone.
Let her finish her work.

LIKE/AS

Like is a preposition; **as** is a subordinating conjunction.
The town clerk acts *like* a dictator.
Her staff does not perform *as* it once did.

PERSPECTIVE/ PROSPECTIVE

Perspective means "viewpoint."
Prospective means "possible."
What is your *perspective* on the buy-out?
We have several *prospective* buyers.

PRECEDE/PROCEED

Precede means "come before."
Proceed means "continue."
The sales talk will *precede* the slide show.
Let's *proceed* with the program.

RAISE/RISE

As a verb, **raise** means "bring up."
Rise means "go up."

Raise and Rise

Present	Past	Present/Past/Future Perfect
raise	raised	raised
rise	rose	risen

Fig. 5.12

Did the executive *raise* any objections?
How did he *rise* to such a high position?

SET/SIT

Set means "place."
Sit means "settle upright."

Set and Sit

Present	**Past**	**Present/Past/Future Perfect**
set	set	set
sit	sat	sat

Fig. 5.13

Set the computer boxes in the corner.
The computer will *sit* on that desk.

6

Capitalization and Punctuation

- Capital Letters
- End Punctuation
- Periods in Initials and Abbreviations
- Commas
- Semicolons
- Colons
- Apostrophes
- Quotation Marks
- Dashes and Ellipses
- Hyphens and Solidi
- Parentheses and Brackets
- Underlines and Italics
- Proofreading

If grammar is the vehicle by which language moves, capitalization and punctuation are the linchpins that hold the vehicle together. Consider the following examples and their differences in meaning:

I ask, "Dad, to pick roses, do you wear gloves?"
I ask Dad to pick roses. Do you wear gloves?
I ask Dad to pick roses. Do you? Wear gloves!
I ask Dad, "To pick roses, do you wear gloves?"

CAPITAL LETTERS

- Capitalize the **first word of a sentence.**

We drew up our plans for the new building.

This rule applies when the sentence is part of a *direct quotation* or follows a *colon.*

He said, "This could be a difficult task."
The manual clearly states: Ask for assistance.

- Capitalize the **first word of each line of a poem.**

Shall I compare thee to a summer's day?
Thou art more lovely and more temperate:
Rough winds do shake the darling buds of May,
And summer's lease hath all too short a date. . . .

- Capitalize the **first word of a letter's salutation or closing.**

Dear Ms. Barthold:

Sincerely yours,

- Capitalize the **first word of an enacting or resolving clause.**

Resolved by the Assembly of New York, That . . .
Be it enacted, That . . .

- Capitalize the **pronoun *I*.**

Marcy and I wrote that catalog copy.

- Capitalize **proper nouns that name people.**

Jerome **Lucy Alvarez** **John Jacob Astor**

Titles of people are capitalized when they precede a name.

Aunt Helen **Chairperson Lee** **Doctor Robb**

However, they are not capitalized if they merely identify people.

I visited my aunt. **The chairperson spoke.**

Names of members of specific organizations are capitalized.

Boy Scout **Libertarian** **Special Olympian**

Capitalize **proper nouns that name places.**

Lake Erie **San José** **Main Street**

Regions, localities, and geographic features are capitalized.

the Middle East **the Western Hemisphere** **the Adirondacks**

However, directional words are not.

eastern **southward** **north**

In a few specific instances, the article that precedes a place name is capitalized.

The Gambia **El Salvador** **Los Angeles**

Capitalize **proper nouns that name things.**

Thanksgiving ***Animal Farm*** **Swahili**

Months, days, and holidays are capitalized.

April **Monday** **Halloween**

However, seasons are not.

fall **winter** **springtime**

Historic events are capitalized.

the Renaissance **War of 1812** **Battle of the Bulge**

Trade names are capitalized.

Bosco **Xerox** **Kleenex tissues**

Names of organizations are capitalized.

Department of Defense **the Congress**
First Federal Bank **Cornell University**

Titles of publications, documents, and laws are capitalized.

***Time* magazine** **the Constitution** **Public Law 150**

Specific references to parts of documents are capitalized.

Chapter 9 **Appendix C** **Amendment XIV**

- Capitalize certain **proper adjectives.**

Jacobean **Himalayan** **Russian**

Possessive proper nouns used as adjectives are capitalized.

Parkinson's law **Raynaud's disease**

However, do not capitalize adjectives that have found their way over time into use as common adjectives.

brussels sprouts **roman numeral** **venetian blinds**

Do not capitalize adjectives that do not refer to specific proper names.

congressional approval **presidential power**

Do not capitalize directional adjectives unless they are parts of proper names.

west Hoboken **West Indies**

END PUNCTUATION

Use a **period** to end a **declarative sentence.**

I told Doctor James about the meeting.

Use a **period** to end an **imperative sentence.**

Remember your notebook.
Please remove that sign.

Use a **question mark** to end an **interrogative sentence.**

What is today's date?

Use an **exclamation point** to end an **exclamatory sentence.**

What a remarkable speaker she is!

PERIODS IN INITIALS AND ABBREVIATIONS

Use a **period** after an **initial.**

E. B. White **Susan B. Anthony** **H. Ross Perot**

Use a **period** with most **abbreviations.**

Mr. **P.M.** **Oct. 31** **Co.** **Ave.**

Postal abbreviations require no periods.

Albany, NY **Washington, DC** **Butte, MT**

Some organizations, agencies, and businesses require no periods. The new U.S. postal codes prefer all capital letters and no punctuation on address labels. (See page 202 for examples.) Some organizations, agencies, and businesses require no periods.

AFL-CIO MIT NASA AT&T FDA

Metric measurements require no periods.

230 m 40 g kW mL

When in doubt, check a dictionary.

COMMAS

- Use **commas** to separate three or more **items in a series.**

with nouns	**We ordered paper, disks, and binders.**
with adjectives	**I prefer those heavy, red, two-ply folders.**
with phrases	**The firm processed our order, shipped it, and billed us immediately.**

Two or more adjectives preceding a noun usually require a comma to separate them.

I prefer the heavy, red folders.

Series that include more than one conjunction take no commas.

Paper and disks and binders are essential.

Never use a comma before an ampersand in the name of a firm.

Biggs, Chardun & Roper Valdez, Chung, Hals & Lee

- Use a **comma** to separate **independent clauses joined by a conjunction.**

The CEO arrived, and she and Mr. Jensen went to lunch.
They reviewed the plan, but it seemed unworkable.
It may go back to the committee, or it may be scrapped.
We hope it is accepted, for we put in a lot of effort.

If there is no conjunction, use a **semicolon** instead.

> **They reviewed the plan; it seemed unworkable.**

If the conjunction simply joins two predicates, no comma is required.

> **The CEO arrived and plans to lunch with Mr. Jensen.**

- Use a **comma** after an **introductory word, phrase, or clause.**

with words	**Yes, I am supervising the new assistant.**
	However, it is not a difficult task.
with phrases	**Barring disaster, she should work out well.**
	For a relatively new employee, she seems terrific.
with clauses	**Unless she leaves, I expect her to be promoted.**
	If I have anything to say about it, she will be.

- Use a **comma** after a set of **two or more prepositional phrases.**

> **In the evening after work, I attended the opera.**

However, a single introductory prepositional phrase of fewer than five words does not require a comma unless it is necessary to clarify meaning.

> **In the evening I attended the opera.**
> **In the evening, gowns glitter on opera-goers.**
> ***[The comma avoids the confusing "evening gowns."]***

(For a list of common prepositions, see Figure 5.4.)

- Use a **comma** to set off **nonrestrictive phrases and clauses.**

restrictive phrase	**All nurses *expecting time off* will receive overtime instead.**

nonrestrictive phrase	**Nurse Purnima,** ***expecting time off,*** **planned a vacation to Portugal.**
restrictive clause	**Employees** ***who work overtime on a regular basis*** **will be rewarded.**
nonrestrictive clause	**Our supervisor,** ***who works overtime on a regular basis,*** **rarely complains.**

Nonrestrictive phrases and clauses are not essential to the meaning of a sentence; they could be omitted without altering the sense. A clause beginning with *that* is almost always restrictive. A clause beginning with *which* is almost always nonrestrictive.

- Use a **comma** to set off **nouns of direct address.**

Ms. Farkas, did you send that fax?
I hope, my friends, that you understood the memo.
Are there any questions, Professor?

- Use **commas** to set off **interrupters.**

Frankly, this office is a mess.
It looks, in fact, quite dreadful.
We could clean up, of course.

- Use **commas** to set off **appositives and appositive phrases.**

Mr. Mahoney, the president of Cruxform, is in the lobby.
["The president of Cruxform" renames "Mr. Mahoney."]
A brilliant chemist, Mr. Mahoney founded Cruxform in 1985.
["A brilliant chemist" renames "Mr. Mahoney."]
We enjoy talking to Mr. Mahoney, a fascinating storyteller.
["A fascinating storyteller" renames "Mr. Mahoney."]

However, some one-word appositives are so closely allied to the noun they rename that they require no comma.

the painter Dali	**my brother Peter**

• Use **commas** to set off **direct quotations.**

She inquired, "Where might I find the manager?"
"Usually," I explained, "he takes an early lunch."
"I would like to make an appointment," she replied.

• Use a **comma** between certain elements in a **date.**

February 17, 1955 **Monday, March 15**

If a date appears within a sentence, a comma follows it.

On July 4, 1776, an unprecedented event occurred.

• Use a **comma** between certain elements in an **address** within the text of a letter, but not on an envelope.

Freeville, New York **Paris, France**

If an address appears within a sentence, a comma follows it.

The letter from Duluth, Minnesota, is on your desk.

If a mailing address appears within a sentence, commas separate the street address from the city and the city from the state. No comma appears before a ZIP code.

She lives at 11 Pell Place, City Island, New York 10464.

• Use a **comma** after certain elements in a **letter.**

Dear Judy, **Sincerely yours,**

However, in a business letter, use a colon after the salutation.

• Use a **comma** between a name and a **degree, title, or abbreviation.**

Henry Biddle, Esq. **Katy Fenton, M.D.**
Jack Wise, Jr. **Dropnet, Inc.**

• Use **commas** between the **periods of a numeral.**

2,300 **14,076** **$3,422,000**

Never use a comma in a four-digit year, a telephone number, a ZIP code, a fraction, a serial number or in a mailing address.

1995 273-4392 14850 1/2000 No. 103344 CHESTER PA

European correspondence may use periods or spaces in place of commas.

2.300 **14.076** **$3 422 000**

SEMICOLONS

• Use a **semicolon** to separate **independent clauses not joined by a conjunction.**

A fight erupted at the meeting; no one wanted to concede.

Semicolons always appear outside quotation marks.

He shouted, "This is unfair!"; everyone ignored him.

• Use a **semicolon** to separate **independent clauses joined by transitional words.**

We asked for a vote; however, nobody was ready.
The chair moved to adjourn; instead, people milled about.

Most transitional words could be considered either interrupters or introductory words (introducing the second independent clause); therefore, they are followed by commas. Here is a list of some transitional words and phrases.

Transitional Words

as a rule	for example	for instance
furthermore	hence	however
if necessary	in addition	in fact
instead	moreover	nevertheless
of course	that is	therefore

Fig. 6.1

• Use a **semicolon** to separate **independent clauses that contain commas,** even if the clauses are joined by a conjunction.

We requested faxes, letters, or phone calls; but he chose to send a telex.

• Use **semicolons** to separate three or more **items in a series** when those items contain commas.

They met on May 1, 1992; May 16, 1993; and July 13, 1994.

COLONS

• Use a **colon** to precede **a list of items.**

You will need the following materials: a steno pad, a pencil, and a tape recorder.

Never use a colon directly after a verb or preposition.

We called Ms. Vasquez, Mr. Loew, and Mrs. Roberts.
They went through papers, back issues, and files.

• Use a **colon** to precede a **long, formal quotation.**

The director had this to say: "I regret that some of you will need to look for employment in other divisions. It appears that our small department will soon be moved to the Cincinnati plant."

• Use a **colon** to introduce a **complete sentence.**

We know the primary rule: Never complain.
The question is on the table: Who will lead us?

• Use a **colon** after the salutation in a **business letter.**

Dear Captain Fry: **To Whom It May Concern:**

• Use a colon to separate hours and minutes in **time references.**

3:45 **11:15 P.M.** **8:20**

• Use a **colon** to separate chapter and verse in a **Biblical citation** or volume and page in a **journal reference.**

Matthew 3:4 ***Journal of Reading*** **4:421–425**

• Use a **colon** to separate place of publication and publisher in a **bibliographic reference.**

Adams, Helen. *ABCs of Writing*. New York: Cooper Press, 1994.

APOSTROPHES

• Use an **apostrophe** and an *s* to form the **possessive of a singular noun.**

one week's salary **the factory's product**
our class's homework **Ms. Odets's office**

• Use an **apostrophe** alone to form the **possessive of a plural noun that ends in *s*.**

two weeks' salary	**the factories' products**
our classes' homework	**the Odetses' offices**

• Use an apostrophe and an *s* to form the **possessive of a plural noun that does not end in *s*.**

the men's locker room	**the people's decision**

• Use an **apostrophe** and an *s* to form the **possessive of an indefinite pronoun.**

everybody's work	**neither's opinion**

Never use an apostrophe in a possessive personal pronoun.

its production	**letters of hers**

See Figures 5.2 and 5.6 for lists of personal and indefinite pronouns.

• Use an **apostrophe** in the **last word** of a **compound noun**, of the name of an **organization,** or of nouns indicating **joint possession.**

the sergeant-at-arms' duty	**the chief executive's plan**
Bank One's report	**Houghton Mifflin's books**
Dan and Evelyn's company	**interns and clerks' concerns**

However, if the second word is a possessive pronoun, use an apostrophe in the *first word* even if joint possession is indicated.

Dan's and my plan	**interns' and our concerns**

• Use an **apostrophe** in **each noun** in a phrase indicating **independent possession.**

Dan's and Evelyn's meals	**interns' and clerks' jobs**

• Use an **apostrophe** when a possessive noun is used as the **object of a preposition.**

He is an employee of Ken's.
She is a neighbor of the Smiths'.

• Use an **apostrophe** when a noun **precedes a gerund.**

We want to be ready in case of Jed's retiring early.
The club's financing of the trip was appreciated.

• Use an **apostrophe** to indicate the omission of letters or numerals in **contractions.**

you're	**o'clock**	**'39**
[*you are*]	**[*of the clock*]**	**[*1939*]**

In general, avoid contractions in formal writing.

• Use an **apostrophe** and an *s* to form the plural of letters, numbers, symbols, and words referred to as words.

Mind your *p*'s and *q*'s.	**Temperatures are in the 60's.**
Include the +'s and -'s.	**Change all *which*'s to *that*'s.**

This is a subjective rule. *The Chicago Manual of Style* (the University of Chicago Press), for instance, recommends forming the plural by adding *s* with no apostrophe to all numerals and to most words as words. If your company has a stylebook, follow it. If not, choose a rule and be consistent about using it.

QUOTATION MARKS

• Use **quotation marks** to enclose a direct quotation.

"This is a fine organization," I boasted.

Never use quotation marks to enclose an indirect quotation.

I insist that this is a fine organization.

Capitalize the first word in a direct quotation.

He exclaimed, "That is a great tie!"

Do not capitalize the second half of a quoted sentence when the sentence is divided by an interrupter.

"I think," said George, "that you need a vacation."

Set off a quotation with a comma, question mark, or exclamation point.

"Here is our new cafeteria," she announced.
"Isn't it beautiful?" she asked.
"What an enormous room!" he cried.

Put commas and periods inside closing quotation marks.

"He seems nice," said May, "but I hear he can be fierce."

Put semicolons and colons outside closing quotation marks.

She said, "I love this place"; what did she mean?
These words appear in the "Company Motto": ***polite, caring, generous.***

Put question marks and exclamation points inside closing quotation marks when the quotation is a question or exclamation.

"Did you sleep well?" asked Ms. Lowe.
"I always do!" I exclaimed.

Put question marks and exclamation points outside closing quotation marks when the sentence itself is a question or exclamation.

Why did you remark, "That's all there is"?
How odd it was to hear him say, "Don't cry for me"!

Use single quotation marks to enclose a quotation within a direct quotation.

"Didn't you hear me say 'Go away'?" I asked crossly.

Begin a new paragraph each time the speaker changes.

"Did you have time to read the brochure?" Ms. Min asked her new assistant.
"Yes," he answered. "It was very helpful."

Quotations of more than one paragraph require quotation marks at the beginning of each paragraph and the end of the complete quotation.

- Use **quotation marks** to enclose **slang expressions, nicknames,** or **specified terms.**

As we say uptown, you seem to want to "dis" me.
I'd like you to meet Dan "The Man" Harris.
Why did your memo read "eyes only"?
The column labeled "Rules of Conduct" may apply here.

- Use **quotation marks** to enclose **titles** of articles, chapters, editorials, essays, headings, lectures, papers, short poems, short stories, and songs.

I recently read "Rules of Management" in *Forbes*.
Can you remember the words to "Joe Hill"?

DASHES AND ELLIPSES

• Use an **em dash** (indicated in typing as two hyphens: --) to show an **abrupt pause or change** in thought.

> **I asked him—are you listening?—to meet with us.**

• Use an **em dash** to indicate **an unfinished thought.**

> **It was not the best proposal I'd—**

If this occurs within a direct quotation, use a comma after the dash.

> **"It was not the best proposal I'd—," she started to say.**

• Use an **em dash** in place of **commas or parentheses** to clarify meaning.

> **The unforgivable thing—to me, at least—is his failure to praise us for a job well done.**

• Use an **em dash** before a **final clause that summarizes** a list.

> **Renata, Michael, and Wally—these are our top salespeople this month.**

• Use an **em dash** before a **phrase or clause that elaborates or explains** what precedes it.

> **I worked hard on the project—a project that could multiply our profits more than 20 times.**

• Use an **em dash** before a **credit line.**

> **I think that I shall never see**
> **A poem as lovely as a tree.**
>
> **—Joyce Kilmer**

• Use an **en dash** (indicated in typing as one hyphen:–) to indicate **inclusive numbers.**

1992–1995 **pp. 215–16** **6:15–7:15**

• Use **ellipses** to indicate **material omitted from a quotation.**

"Perchance he for whom this bell tolls . . . knows not it tolls for him. . . ."

If the omission includes the end of a sentence, include a period in the ellipsis, making four dots in all. However, if the quoted sentence is not a complete sentence as it stands, use only three dots, leaving the period out.

"The church is catholic, universal. . . ."
"If a clod be washed away by the sea . . ."

• Use **ellipses** to indicate material omitted from a **mathematical expression.**

1, 2, 3, . . . , 9, 10

(For more on punctuation in mathematics, see Chapter 9.)

HYPHENS AND SOLIDI

• Use a **hyphen** to connect parts of **compound words.**

sister-in-law **one-half** **ex-employee**

• Use a **hyphen** between unrelated words used as a **single modifier.**

good-faith agreement **state-of-the-art device**

- Use a **hyphen** to indicate **word division** at the end of a line of type.

Without further ado we marched in-
to the conference room.

(See Chapter 7 for information on dividing words correctly.)

- Use a **solidus** (slash) to indicate **inclusive years.**

summer 1981/1982 **fiscal period 1995/1996**

- Use a **solidus** to indicate a **fraction.**

1/4 ***2a/9b*** **12/360**

In general, stack fractions to eliminate ambiguity unless there is no room to do so.

$\frac{1}{4}$ $\frac{2a}{9b}$ $\frac{12}{360}$

- Use a **solidus** to mean **"per."**

35 km/h **8 ft/sec**

- Use a **solidus** in some **abbreviations** and to **indicate choice.**

c/o Marie Rudd **shipping and/or handling fees**

- Use a **solidus** to mark the **end of a line of poetry** in run-in text.

Milton begins his great work, "Of man's first disobedience, and the fruit/Of that forbidden tree . . ."

PARENTHESES AND BRACKETS

• Use **parentheses** to enclose **information that is not vital** to the meaning of a sentence.

elaborating	**The letter I wrote (under considerable pressure) did not have the desired effect.**
explanatory	**The letter I wrote (the one to my supervisor) did not have the desired effect.**
digressive	**The letter I wrote (as you'll recall, I write splendid letters) did not have the desired effect.**

If the words in parentheses form a sentence of their own, capitalize and punctuate that sentence within the parentheses. If they do not, put any end punctuation outside the close parenthesis.

I wrote a letter. (It was quite brilliant, I think.)
I wrote a letter (of great brilliance and tact).

• Use **parentheses** to enclose **numerals** or **letters** that indicate parts of a list or parts of a text.

Read the first chapter (pages 3–15).
The author states (a) that he is a great man, (b) that he knows everything about business, and (c) that anyone who follows his suggestions will succeed.

• Use **parentheses** to enclose a **restatement of an amount.**

The distance is about three feet (one meter).
It cost approximately one billion dollars ($1,000,000,000).

• Use **brackets** to enclose **material added** by someone other than the original speaker.

Spenser refers to a woman "of wondrous beauty, and of bountie [virtue] rare."

• Use **brackets** when an item in parentheses **requires additional parentheses.** The brackets should be on the outside.

> **The brochure [which Fran completed (her staff were no help at all)] was finished on time.**

• Use **brackets** to enclose **phonetic respellings**.

> **The patient suffers from nephrosis [ni'-frō-ses].**

UNDERLINES AND ITALICS

Underlining and italicizing are essentially the same thing. Traditionally in published works, an underscore has been used to tell a printer to set that type in italics. If your typewriter or word processor does not have italic print, an underscore is just as good. Even if you are able to italicize using your printer, your company stylebook may ask you to underline instead as a matter of consistency and simplicity.

• Use **underlining or italics** for **titles** of books, journals, magazines, movies, long musical works, newspapers, paintings, plays, and long poems.

> **The movie Working Girl made me laugh aloud.**
> **Look at the want ads in the *Washington Post*.**

• Use **underlining or italics** to indicate **words as words, letters as letters,** or **numbers as numbers.**

> **The word existence has more e's than I had guessed.**
> **When he writes a *7*, it has a crossbar.**

• Use **underlining or italics** to indicate **foreign words and abbreviations.**

> **When he says bonjour, be sure to answer politely.**
> **The languages he speaks (*e.g.*, French) are many.**

Genus and species names are in Latin, and as such, they are always underlined or italicized.

> **Dr. Wu recommends an extract of horehound (*Marrubium vulgare*).**

However, names of phyla, classes, orders, and families are not.

> **She is studying wombats, members of the order Marsupialia.**

- Use **underlining or italics** for **legal cases.**

> **Was Brown v. Board of Education the first case you read?**

The *v.*, meaning *versus,* may be underlined or italicized as well, or it may be left in roman type. Check your firm's stylebook, and be consistent.

PROOFREADING

After you draft any document, reread it carefully, checking for errors in capitalization and punctuation, formatting, spelling, syntax, grammar and usage, consistency of style, and overall sense. You may wish to use the standardized system developed by professional proofreaders to prepare your draft for retyping.

Proofreading Marks

symbol	meaning	example
∧	insert	Where did the profits ∧ ? (go)
	delete	Where did the the profits go?
STET	leave as it was	Where did the profits go? (STET)
/	lowercase	Where did the Profits go?
≡	capitalize	where did the profits go?
	spell out	Ask our (U.S.) Senators.
	transpose letters	Aks our United States senators.
⊙	add a period	Ask our U.S⊙ senators.
∧ ,	add a comma	Write to Washington∧, DC.
∧ ;	add a semicolon	I did; they wrote back right away.
∧ :	add a colon	I asked: Where did the profits go?
∨ '	add an apostrophe	I'd never written such a letter.
∨ "	add quotation marks	I asked, "Where did the profits go?"
1/M	add an em dash	The profits 1/M one surmises 1/M are gone.
1/N	add an en dash	The years 1991 1/N 1992 saw no growth.
=	add a hyphen	The ex=president was no help.

symbol	meaning	example
⫞ ⫟	add parentheses	He ⫞the former president⫟ was a lame duck.
⁀‿	close up	My congress person responded.
#	add space	My congresspersonresponded.
¶	indent paragraph	¶My congressperson responded. I am quite grateful for that, and I immediately wrote to thank her.
‖	align	My congressperson responded. I am quite grateful for that, and I immediately wrote to thank her.
⮎	transpose words	My congressperson responded. I am quite grateful for that, and I immediately wrote to thank her.
bf	boldface	She is genuinely responsive.
ITAL	italicize	The word caring comes to mind.

Fig. 6.2

7

Spelling and Word Division

- Pronunciation and Spelling
- Word Meaning and Spelling
- Silent Letters
- *EI/IE*
- Plurals
- Prefixes
- Suffixes
- Homophones
- Frequently Misspelled Words
- Word Division

Good spelling counts. Any correspondence or material that has misspelled words looks sloppy. A letter with spelling mistakes says that the writer didn't care enough to check on words he or she didn't know, or might have mistyped. Most word processing programs now contain a spelling function that checks the spelling in a document, but that program will not differentiate between frequently confused words such as *stationary* and *stationery*. And, for every spelling rule in English, there is an exception. Your best bet is always to have a good dictionary close at hand. When in doubt, look it up.

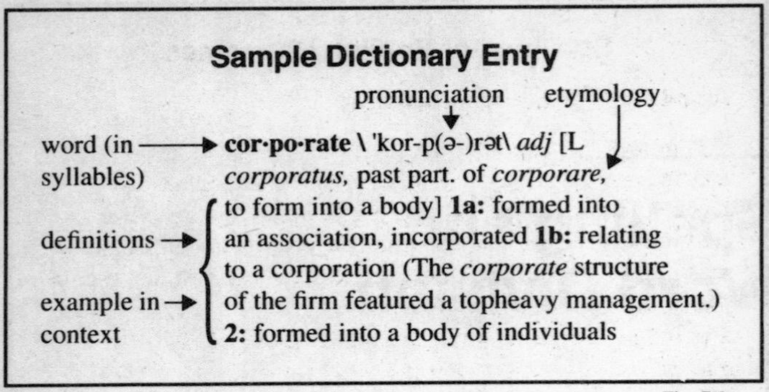

Sample Dictionary Entry

pronunciation etymology

word (in syllables) → **cor·po·rate** \ 'kor-p(ə-)rət\ *adj* [L *corporatus,* past part. of *corporare,* to form into a body] **1a:** formed into an association, incorporated **1b:** relating to a corporation (The *corporate* structure of the firm featured a topheavy management.) **2:** formed into a body of individuals

definitions →

example in context →

Fig. 7.1

PRONUNCIATION AND SPELLING

If you pronounce a word incorrectly, you are likely to spell it incorrectly as well. Are you guilty of these common errors?

athelete* instead of *athlete
Febuary* instead of *February
mischievious* instead of *mischievous
temperture* instead of *temperature

If you frequently drop letters or add syllables when you spell, your problem may be one of pronunciation. Study the pronunciation guide when you look up a word in your dictionary. Notice how the word breaks into syllables. Then use that as your guide in spelling the word.

Every phoneme, or sound, in English has a variety of spellings. Here are some possible spellings for a variety of phonemes. The list is by no means complete, but it will give you an idea of the possibilities and show you what you are up against each time you set out to spell an unfamiliar word.

Spellings of English Phonemes

sound	possible spellings
a as in *rain*	a, a-e, ai, au, ay, é, ea, ei, eigh, et, ey
e as in *meet*	ae, ay, e, ea, ee, ei, eo, ey, ie, i-e, oe
i as in *ice*	ai, ei, eigh, ey, eye, i, i-e, ie, igh, uy, y, ye
o as in *okay*	au, eau, ew, o, oa, oe, o-e, oh, oo, ou, ough, ow
u as in *flu*	eu, ew, o, oe, o-e, oo, ou, ough, u, ue, u-e, ui
f as in *fan*	f, ff, gh, ph
k as in *kite*	c, cc, ch, ck, cq, cu, k, kh, q, qu
z as in *zoo*	s, ss, x, z, zz
sh as in *shut*	ce, ch, ci, s, sch, sci, sh, si, ss, ssi, ti

Fig. 7.2

WORD MEANING AND SPELLING

Like people, words come in families. If you recognize the family of an unfamiliar word, you are on the way to spelling it correctly. Often the key to identifying a word's family is to determine its meaning.

Suppose the unfamiliar word on your dictation cassette sounds something like *pressident.* You know from the context on the tape that a *pressident,* in the legal paper you are typing, is a case that came before the case now being decided. In other words, it *preceded* the case. So, in context, it's clear that *precede* is related to the unfamiliar *pressident.* If you can spell *precede,* you can spell your unfamiliar word correctly: *precedent.*

SILENT LETTERS

Your ability to pronounce correctly means nothing when your unfamiliar word contains a silent letter.

- The letter most often silent in English is ***e***. Many one-syllable words with long vowel sounds are formed using the vowel plus silent *e*.

cape **theme** **pine** **note** **cute**

Without the silent *e*, the words above would be *cap, them, pin, not,* and *cut*—words with very different pronunciations and meanings.

- When ***b*** is silent, it follows *m*.

comb **lamb** **thumb**

However, there are times when *b* follows *m* and is not silent.

iambic

- When ***n*** is silent, it follows *m*.

autumn **column** **limn**

However, there are times when *n* follows *m* and is not silent.

autumnal **hymnal**

This is a case where knowing a related word—*autumnal*—may help you spell the word with a silent letter—*autumn.*

- When ***k*** is silent, it precedes *n*.

knapsack **know** **knuckle**

Many silent letters follow no apparent rules. They are often leftovers from the foreign language from which the word is derived. Often the etymology section of the entry in your dictionary will give you clues about this.

EI/IE

The old, familiar rule "*i* before *e* except after *c*" does not tell the whole story.

- If the sound is ***e* as in *meet*, write *ie*.**

ach**ie**ve	bel**ie**f	p**ie**ce

However, if *i* and *e* come **after *c*, write *ei*.**

c**ei**ling	dec**ei**t

As with all spelling rules, this one has exceptions. Here are a few of them.

either	s**ei**zure	w**ei**rd

- If the sound is ***a* as in *rain*, write *ei*.**

n**eigh**bor	r**ei**n	w**eigh**

- If the sound is a short vowel, it could go either way.

fr**ie**nd	handkerch**ie**f	misch**ie**vous
counterf**ei**t	for**ei**gn	forf**ei**ture

PLURALS

- Form the plural of most nouns by adding **-*s*.**

park	parks	rate	rates

- Form the plural of nouns ending in *ch, sh, s, ss, x, z,* or *zz* by adding ***-es*.**

peach	peaches	rash	rashes
bus	buses	pass	passes
fox	foxes	Cortez	Cortezes
buzz	buzzes		

• Form the plural of nouns ending in a consonant and *o* by adding ***-es***.

hero	heroes	potato	potatoes

However, if a vowel precedes the *o,* just add *-s*.

radio	radios	stereo	stereos

If the noun relates to music, just add *-s*.

alto	altos	virtuoso	virtuosos

• Form the plural of nouns ending in a consonant or *qu* and *y* by **changing the *y* to *i* and adding *-es*.**

baby	babies	soliloquy	soliloquies

However, if the noun ends in a vowel and *y*, just add *-s*.

monkey	monkeys	play	plays

Never change *y* to *i* in a proper noun. Just add *-s*.

January	Januarys	Mary	Marys

• Form the plural of some nouns ending in *f* or *fe* by **changing the *f* to *v* and adding *-s* or *-es*.**

leaf	leaves	knife	knives

However, many nouns ending in *f* or *fe* do not follow this rule.

roof	roofs	fife	fifes

• Use an **apostrophe** and an *s* to form the plural of letters, numbers, symbols, and words referred to as words.

o	*o*'s	#	#'s

lany irregular nouns follow no rules at all in the formation of lurals. You must simply memorize these nouns. Here are some xamples, arranged by type.

Irregular Plural Nouns

man men	woman women		goose geese	tooth teeth	foot feet
deer deer	fish fish	sheep sheep	ox oxen	child children	
mouse mice			bacterium bacteria	datum data	
index indices	appendix appendices		phenomenon phenomena	criterion criteria	
crisis crises	thesis theses		radius radii	stimulus stimuli	

Fig. 7.3

REFIXES

A prefix is a letter or letters added to the beginning of a word r root to alter the word's meaning. There are a few spelling ules related to prefixes.

If the prefix is ***all-, ex-,* or *self-,*** use a **hyphen** between the refix and the base word.

all-encompassing **ex**-president **self**-explanatory

If the prefix **precedes a proper noun or numeral,** use a **hy-hen** between the prefix and the base word.

un-American **pre**-1900

• If the prefix creates a word that **might be confused with a homonym or might be misread,** use a **hyphen** between the prefix and the base word.

re-creation	**un-**ionized
re-enter	**anti-**inflammatory

Here is a list of commonly used prefixes.

Common Prefixes

prefix	meaning	example
a-	not	atypical
all-	completely	all-American
ante-	before	antecedent
anti-	against	antibiotic
auto-	self	autobiography
bi-	two	binomial
co-	with	coauthor
com-, con-	with	companion, context
contra-	against	contradict
counter-	against	counterclockwise
de-	from	devalue
dis-	not, opposite of	distrust
ex-	out of, former	exhale, ex-employee
extra-	outside, beyond	extraordinary
fore-	before	forewarn
il-, im-	not	illogical, impolite,
in-, ir-		incorrect, irregular

[Notice that il- *is used before words that begin with* l, *and* ir- *is used before words that begin with* r.*]*

prefix	meaning	example
inter-	between	international
intra-	within	intracellular
macro-	large	macroeconomics
micro-	small	microscope

prefix	meaning	example
mid-	central	midyear
mis-	wrong	misname
multi-	many	multicolored
non-	not	nonmember
over-	above, excessively	overdeveloped
post-	after	postdoctoral
pre-	before	prefabricated
pro-	forward, for	promotion, pro-art
pseudo-	false	pseudoscience
re-	again	rewrite
semi-	half, partly	semicircle
sub-	below	submarine
super-	above	superintendent
trans-	across	transcontinental
ultra-	beyond	ultraconservative
un-	not	unequal
under-	below, less than optimally	underreported

Fig. 7.4

SUFFIXES

A suffix is a letter or letters added to the end of a word or root to alter the word's meaning and often its part of speech. Many of the rules for adding suffixes also apply to the addition of inflected endings such as *-ing* or *-ed*.

- **Double a consonant** before adding an ending if the one-syllable root word ends in a single consonant and contains one vowel.

hit hi**tt**ing shop sho**pp**ed

• **Double a consonant** before adding an ending if the multi-syllable word ends in a single consonant preceded by a vowel and the accent falls on the last syllable.

compel	compe**lling**	occur	occu**rred**

Your company may have exceptions to this rule in its stylebook. Some stylebooks, for example, recommend *travelled* rather than *traveled,* despite the fact that the accent is on the first syllable. Memorize any exceptions of this sort.

• If the suffix begins with a consonant, **retain the silent *e*** on the end of the root word.

hate	hate**ful**	polite	polite**ly**

However, some words with a soft *g* sound drop the *e*.

judge	judg**ment**	acknowledge	acknowledg**ment**

Words that end in two vowels drop the *e*.

true	tru**ly**	undue	undu**ly**

• If the suffix begins with a vowel, **drop the silent *e*** on the end of the root word.

love	lov**able**	please	pleas**ant**

However, keep the silent *e* if it eliminates confusion.

dye	dy**eing** [*not* dying]

Retain the silent *e* if it is preceded by a soft *c* or *g*, unless the suffix begins with *i*.

change	chang**eable** [*but* changing]

• If the root word ends in *y* preceded by a consonant, **change the *y* to *i*** before adding a suffix, unless the suffix begins with *i*.

nasty	nast**ily**	hurry	hurr**ying**

Here is a list of commonly used suffixes.

Common Suffixes

suffix	meaning	example
-able, -ible	able to, capable of	washable, divisible
-an	one that is of	Asian
-ance, -ence	state of	annoyance, independence
-en, -n	make	lengthen, whiten
-er, -or	one who	writer, sailor
-ful	full of	careful
-ian	one skilled in	musician
-ic	like, characterized by	heroic
-ion, -sion, -tion	state, result of	tension, extension, reduction
-ish	like, suggesting	waspish
-ism	practice of	Hinduism
-ist	one who practices	flutist
-ite	native of	Brooklynite
-ity, -ty	condition of	reality, certainty
-ive	relating to	assertive
-ize, -yze	causing	alphabetize, analyze
-less	lacking	helpless
-ly	in a way	patiently
-ment	state, result of	judgment
-ness	state, condition of	sweetness
-ology	study of	anthropology
-ous	in a condition of	joyous
-self	self	herself
-ward	in the direction of	backward
-y	suggesting	smoky

Fig. 7.5

There are no good, reliable spelling rules to help you choose the correct suffix for a given root word—is it *ance* or *ence? er* or *or?* Again, often the answer lies in long-forgotten etymology. When in doubt, consult your dictionary.

HOMOPHONES

BARE/BEAR	**Bare** means "naked"; **bear** is an animal, or it means "carry." Those are the *bare* facts of the case. The *bear* entered the park on the road. Can you *bear* the burden?
CAPITAL/CAPITOL	**Capital** is a city or assets, or it is an adjective meaning either "excellent" or "punishable by execution." **Capitol** is a statehouse. Albany is New York's *capital.* We used the *capital* to buy machines. You did a *capital* job on the report. Is kidnapping a *capital* crime? The dome of the *capitol* shines.
CITE/SIGHT/SITE	To **cite** is to quote. To **sight** is to see. To **site** is to situate. He will *cite* Luther in his speech. I can *sight* the tower from here. Let's *site* the house on the hilltop.
COMPLEMENT/ COMPLIMENT	**Complement** means "fulfill" or "add to." **Compliment** means "praise" or "commend." The rug will nicely *complement* the room. I must *compliment* the decorator.

COUNCIL/COUNSEL A **council** is a group of people.
Counsel means "advice" or "advise."
The city *council* meets on Tuesdays.
She will *counsel* us on tax planning.

FORWARD/FOREWORD **Forward** is a direction; a **foreword** is a preface.
Move *forward* in the checkout line.
Skim the *foreword* of the manual.

ITS/IT'S **Its** is a possessive pronoun.
It's is short for "it is."
My company treats *its* workers well.
It's an ideal place in which to work.

LIABLE/LIBEL **Liable** means "likely."
Libel is a form of defamation.
He is *liable* to take that badly.
He may sue you for *libel*.

LIGHTENING/LIGHTNING **Lightening** is the act of making lighter.
Lightning is atmospheric electricity.
She is *lightening* her hair color.
Lightning struck the old barn.

MANNER/MANOR **Manner** means "way"; a **manor** is a large house.
She has an odd *manner* of speaking.
Who will buy the duke's old *manor?*

MINER/MINOR A **miner** works in a mine; **minor** means "underage" or "trivial."
The *miner* came from West Virginia.
No *minor* may purchase liquor.
I made a *minor* change to the document.

PASSED/PAST **Passed** is the past tense of *pass*.
Past means "ago" or "former."

	I *passed* John on the staircase. In the *past* we worked together.
PEACE/PIECE	**Peace** is a state of tranquillity. **Piece** is a portion. The treaty means *peace* is here at last. Have a *piece* of this cherry tart.
PEEK/PIQUE	To **peek** is to glimpse; **pique** is resentment or provocation. Do not *peek* until I have finished. She stalked off in a fit of *pique.*
PLAIN/PLANE	**Plain** means "unadorned" or "prairie." **Plane** means "aircraft" or "level." She wore a *plain* smock. Kansas is mostly *plains* with some hills. We exited the *plane* in Wichita. That firm is on a different *plane* from ours.
PRINCIPAL/ PRINCIPLE	**Principal** is a noun meaning "headmaster" or "capital," or it is an adjective meaning "primary." **Principle** is a noun meaning "rule" or "ethics." The *principal* can tell you about benefits. We invested the *principal* in treasury bonds. That was our *principal* source of income. As a matter of *principle,* we pay very well.
RAIN/REIGN/REIN	To **rain** is to precipitate. To **reign** is to rule.

To **rein** is to control a horse.
Will it *rain* or be sunny today?
The Shah's *reign* ended abruptly.
The coach driver will *rein* in the team.

REEK/WREAK/WRECK

To **reek** is to smell bad. To **wreak** (which may be pronounced to rhyme with *reek* or with *wreck*) is to cause. To **wreck** is to destroy.
The old dogs *reek* when they're wet.
Storms *wreak* havoc on Florida every year.
Smoking may *wreck* your health.

SAIL/SALE

A **sail** is a cruise or a canvas sheet.
A **sale** is an act of trade.
We took a *sail* to Bermuda.
The *sail* flapped in the breeze.
How many items are on *sale?*

STATIONARY/STATIONERY

Stationary means "motionless."
Stationery means "paper goods."
Is the chair on wheels, or is it *stationary?*
Send him a letter on company *stationery*.

THEIR/THERE/THEY'RE

Their is a possessive pronoun.
There is an adverb meaning "in that place."
They're is short for "they are."
Their order got *there,* and *they're* glad.

WHO'S/WHOSE

Who's is short for "who is."
Whose is a possessive pronoun.
Who's on the steering committee?
Whose name is on the list?

YOUR/YOU'RE

Your is a possessive pronoun.
You're is short for "you are."
Was that *your* answering machine?
I guess *you're* not taking any calls.

FREQUENTLY MISSPELLED WORDS

a·ban·don
ab·bre·vi·ate
ab·er·rant
a·bey·ance
ab·hor
a·bil·i·ty
ab·o·li·tion
ab·o·rig·i·ne
ab·rupt
ab·sence
ab·solve
ab·sorp·tion
ab·sten·tion
ab·sti·nent
ac·cel·er·ate
ac·cept·ance
ac·ces·so·ry
ac·ci·den·tal·ly
ac·co·lade
ac·com·pa·nist
ac·cor·di·on
ac·cu·ra·cy
ac·knowl·edge
ac·quaint
ad·dress
ad·e·quate
ad·just·a·ble
af·fi·da·vit
ag·gres·sive
al·be·it
al·co·hol
al·le·giance
am·a·teur
ap·par·ent
ar·gu·ment
as·cend
as·phyx·i·ate
as·pi·rin
as·sas·sin
at·ten·dance
av·er·age
bach·e·lor
bag·gage
band·age
bank·rupt·cy
ban·quet
bar·be·cue
bay·ou
ba·zaar
beau·ty
be·lief
bel·lig·er·ent
ben·e·fit
bi·zarre
blood
bomb
bou·tique
buf·fa·lo
bul·le·tin
buoy·ant
busi·ness
cal·en·dar
cal·i·brate
can·cel
cap·sule
car·riage
cat·e·go·ry
cen·sor
chan·cel·lor
cir·cuit
cli·en·tele
co·in·ci·dence
col·league
col·lect·i·ble
col·lege
com·mit·tee
com·pe·tent
con·fi·dent
con·grat·u·late
con·science
con·tro·ver·sy
con·ven·ient
cor·re·late
crit·i·cize
cu·ri·os·i·ty
debt
de·ceased

dé·col·le·tage
de·co·ra·tor
de·fend·ant
def·in·ite
de·lib·er·ate
de·pend·a·ble
de·pend·ence
des·per·ate
di·ag·o·nal
dif·fi·cult
di·gest·i·ble
diph·the·ri·a
dis·ci·ple
dis·si·pate
doc·ile
dom·i·nant
doubt
ec·ze·ma
ed·i·tor
ef·fi·cient
e·gre·gious
el·e·men·ta·ry
el·i·gi·ble
em·bar·rass
em·bas·sy
em·pha·size
en·dea·vor
en·dur·ance
en·vi·ron·ment
e·piph·a·ny
e·pit·o·me
e·qua·tion
es·pe·cial·ly
ev·i·dence
ex·ag·ger·ate
ex·cel·lent
ex·er·cise
ex·hib·it
ex·ist·ence
ex·or·bi·tant
ex·pen·di·ture
ex·traor·di·nar·y
ex·ult
fa·cil·i·ty
fac·sim·i·le
fas·cist
Feb·ru·ar·y
fel·on
fe·tal
flag·el·late
flam·ma·ble
flu·o·res·cent
for·eign
for·feit
fraud·u·lent
fruit
fu·gi·tive
gal·lop
gauche
gauze
ges·ture
glob·al
gon·or·rhe·a
gouge
gov·ern·ment
grad·u·a·tion
gra·tu·i·ty
griev·ance
gro·tesque
guar·an·tee
guile
gym·na·si·um
ha·be·as cor·pus
hand·some
ha·rass
health
heif·er
height
her·e·tic
hi·a·tus
ho·lis·tic
hon·est
hyp·o·crite
i·den·ti·cal
i·de·o·lo·gy
il·le·gal
il·lu·so·ry
im·me·di·ate
im·mo·bile
im·promp·tu
in·au·gu·ra·tion
in·ci·dent
in·de·pen·dent
in·dict
in·fi·nite
in·her·it·ance
in·te·grate
in·ter·mit·tent
in·ter·pret
in·vis·i·ble
ir·rel·e·vant
is·land
i·tal·i·cize
i·tin·er·ar·y
jag·uar
jav·e·lin
jeal·ous
jeop·ar·dy
jew·el·ry
jour·nal·ism
judg·ment
juice
ju·ve·nile
ki·osk

know·ledge
ku·dos
lab·o·ra·to·ry
la·con·ic
la·i·ty
lar·ynx
law·yer
learn
leg·is·la·ture
le·gi·ti·mate
lei·sure
length
li·cense
li·quor
li·ter
lon·gev·i·ty
lun·cheon
lus·cious
lux·ur·y
lyr·i·cist
mael·strom
mag·ic
mag·ni·fi·cent
main·te·nance
ma·laise
ma·lev·o·lent
ma·lig·nant
man·da·to·ry
man·ne·quin
man·sion
mar·gin
mar·quee
mar·riage
mas·och·ism
math·e·mat·ics
med·i·cine
me·di·o·cre
me·di·um
mil·ieu
mil·len·i·um
min·i·mal
min·ute
mi·rage
mis·cel·la·ne·ous
mis·chie·vous
mis·de·mean·or
mi·sog·y·ny
mis·spell
mne·mon·ic
mo·nop·o·ly
mu·ni·ci·pal
mus·cle
mu·tu·al
na·dir
na·sal
nat·ur·al
nau·seous
nec·es·sar·y
neg·li·gent
ne·go·ti·ate
neu·ro·sis
non·cha·lant
no·ta·ry
nour·ish
nu·cle·us
o·bey
o·blige
ob·scene
ob·sess
oc·ca·sion
oc·cu·pant
oc·cur·rence
o·mis·sion
om·ni·scient
on·o·mat·o·poe·ia
op·er·a·tor
oph·thal·mol·o·gy
op·por·tu·ni·ty
o·pos·sum
op·po·site
or·ches·tra
o·rig·i·nal
os·cil·late
os·ten·si·ble
o·ver·ture
o·ver·whelm
ox·y·gen
pack·age
pag·eant
paid
par·a·digm
par·al·lel
par·cel
pa·tient
pe·cu·liar
pe·des·tri·an
pe·jo·ra·tive
pen·i·cil·lin
pen·sion
per·cen·tile
per·ma·nent
per·sist·ent
per·son·nel
per·suade
pe·ti·tion
phar·ma·ceu·ti·cal
Phil·ip·pines
phy·si·cian
pi·e·ty
play·wright
pleas·ant
poi·son
pos·i·tive
pos·ses·sion

poul·try
prac·ti·cal
pre·cinct
pref·er·ence
pres·by·te·ri·an
pres·tige
pri·ma fa·ci·e
pri·or
pri·vi·lege
pro·ce·dure
pro·fes·sor
pro·le·tar·i·at
pro·nun·ci·a·tion
pro·phy·lac·tic
psy·che
pu·ni·tive
quaff
quan·da·ry
quar·an·tine
quer·u·lous
ques·tion·naire
quix·o·tic
rar·i·ty
ra·tio
rau·cous
re·bel·lion
re·ceive
re·cess
re·cruit
re·demp·tion
re·dun·dant
re·fer·ence
rem·i·nis·cent
re·mu·ner·ate
re·nown
rep·er·toire
req·ui·site
re·scind
res·er·voir
res·tau·rant
res·tau·ra·teur
re·sus·ci·tate
rhap·so·dy
rheu·ma·tism
ris·qué
rit·u·al
ru·mor
ru·ral
sab·o·tage
sac·cha·rine
sa·fa·ri
sanc·tu·ar·y
sav·age
scal·pel
scan·dal
sce·nar·i·o
sched·ule
schiz·o·phre·ni·a
schol·ar
seg·re·gate
sen·a·tor
sep·a·rate
se·quen·tial
sev·er·ance
sher·iff
sign
sig·na·ture
sig·nif·i·cant
sim·i·lar
so·cial
soft·en
sol·emn
so·lil·o·quy
sou·ve·nir
sov·er·eign
spa·tial
spe·cies
spon·sor
squeak
stom·ach
strait·jack·et
strat·e·gy
strict·ly
struc·ture
sub·poe·na
sub·si·dy
suc·cess
suc·cumb
sum·mar·y
su·per·cede
sup·posed
sur·prise
sur·geon
sur·ro·gate
sur·veil·lance
sus·pi·cious
syl·la·ble
sym·me·try
syn·the·size
syr·up
tac·it
tar·iff
tech·ni·cian
ten·don
ten·or
ten·ure
ter·res·tri·al
ter·ri·to·ry
tet·a·nus
the·sau·rus
thief
tho·rough
tol·er·ant
trai·tor

trou·sers	vac·u·um	Wed·nes·day
tu·ber·cu·lo·sis	vague	weird
tyr·an·ny	ve·he·ment	where·as
ul·ti·mate	ven·ue	whol·ly
un·a·bridged	ves·sel	with·hold
u·nan·i·mous	vict·ual	womb
unc·tu·ous	vig·i·lant	wom·en
u·nique	vin·ai·grette	yacht
un·nec·es·sar·y	vi·rus	yearn
u·su·al	vol·a·tile	zeal·ous
u·til·i·ty	vo·yeur	zep·pe·lin
vac·ci·nate	weap·on	zo·o·log·i·cal

WORD DIVISION

The words in the preceding list are broken into syllables, or related units of sound. Your dictionary, too, lists entries with their syllable breaks. This helps you determine how to break a word at the end of a line of type, should you have to do so.

There are a number of rules governing word division.

- Do not divide words of **one syllable.**

me	**mile**	**mosque**

- Do not divide **abbreviations, figures, or numbers.**

NAACP	**10,000**	**ten thousand**

- Do not divide the last word of a paragraph.
- Do not divide **proper nouns.**

David	**January**	**Newark**

• Do not divide words of **six letters or fewer.**

extra	**energy**	**epic**

• Do not divide the **suffixes** *-able, -ceous, -cial, -cion, -qeous, -gion, -gious, -ible, -sial, -sion, -tial, -tion,* or *-tious.* Do not leave any of these suffixes alone at the beginning of a line of text.

incorrect	**curva-/ceous**	***incorrect***	**substanti-/al**
correct	**cur-/vaceous**	***correct***	**sub-/stantial**

• Do not divide words leaving a **two-letter syllable** at the beginning of a line of text.

incorrect	**farmwork-/er**
correct	**farm-/worker**

• Do not divide **diphthongs.**

incorrect	**to-/yshop**
correct	**toy-/shop**

• Divide words containing **prefixes** at the prefix.

dis-/pleased	**un-/happy**	**non-/sensical**

• Divide words containing **double consonants** at the syllable break.

col-/lec-/ted

However, if the word is a root word form, keep the consonants together.

collar

If the double consonant appears before an *-ing* ending, the second consonant stays with the *-ing* ending.

jug-/gling

- Divide **hyphenated** and **compound words** at the hyphen or the full word division.

self-/reliant **boarding-/house**

8

Abbreviations

- Titles and Degrees
- Addresses
- Organizations and Agencies
- Acronyms
- Calendar Divisions
- Text Citations
- Units of Measure

In this chapter, you will see the different kinds of abbreviations you are likely to use on the job. Keep in mind that abbreviations are used to save space or to eliminate the need to spell out repeated words or phrases. Many abbreviations are standard and easily recognized by readers. However, when you use an uncommon abbreviation, first spell out the reference completely with the abbreviation immediately following in parentheses. Then use the abbreviation as needed.

TITLES AND DEGREES

• Abbreviate a **title preceding a name** in all but formal references.

Insp. Gen. Cartwright **Ms.** Chio-chu

You may abbreviate *honorable, reverend,* and *monsignor* unless they are preceded by the word *the.*

Rev. John Simon   the Reverend John Simon

- Abbreviate a **title or degree following a name.**

Roger Wright, **Esq.**   Sunny May, **D.V.M.**

Use a comma between the name and the title. Do not use any introductory title with the title *Esq.* or with any academic degrees.

incorrect	**Dr. Jane Quincey, M.D.**
correct	**Jane Quincey, M.D.**

Common Abbreviations of Titles and Degrees

Adj.	Adjutant
Adm.	Admiral
Atty. Gen.	Attorney General
Brig. Gen.	Brigadier General
Capt.	Captain
Col.	Colonel
Comdr.	Commander
C.P.A.	Certified Public Accountant
Cpl.	Corporal
DA	District Attorney
D.D.	Doctor of Divinity
D.D.S.	Doctor of Dental Science
D.O.	Doctor of Osteopathy
Dr.	Doctor
D.V.M.	Doctor of Veterinary Medicine
Ed.D.	Doctor of Education
Ens.	Ensign
Esq.	Esquire (attorney)
Fr.	Father
1st Lt.	First Lieutenant

Gen.	General
Gov.	Governor
Insp. Gen.	Inspector General
Hon.	Honorable
J.D.	*Jurum Doctor* (Doctor of Law)
J.P.	Justice of the Peace
Jr.	Junior
LL.D.	*Legum Doctor* (Doctor of Laws)
Lt.	Lieutenant
Lt. Col.	Lieutenant Colonel
Lt. Gov.	Lieutenant Governor
M.A.	Master of Arts
Maj.	Major
Maj. Gen.	Major General
M.	*Monsieur*
M.B.A.	Master of Business Administration
M. Div.	Master of Divinity (seminary graduates, ministers)
Messrs.	Misters
Mlle.	*Mademoiselle*
Mme.	*Madame*
M.P.	Member of Parliament
Mr.	Mister
Mrs.	Mistress
Ms.	coined female title
M.S.	Master of Science
Msgr.	Monsignor
Ph.D.	Doctor of Philosophy
P.M.	Prime Minister
Pres.	President
Prof.	Professor
Pvt.	Private
Rep.	Representative
Rev.	Reverend
R.N.	Registered Nurse
Sen.	Senator

Sgt.	Sergeant
Sr.	Senior; Sister
Supt.	Superintendent
Vice Adm.	Vice Admiral

Fig. 8.1

ADDRESSES

In formal writing, spell out all geographic terms. Use abbreviations only in addresses or descriptions of tracts of land. The exceptions, depending on your company stylebook, may be the use of *U.S.* as an adjective, as in *U.S. Mail,* and the use of *St.* or *Ste.* to stand for *Saint,* as in *St. Louis.*

• In addresses for mailing, capitalize all letters and avoid all punctuation except hyphens.

35 MAIN ST **NEWPORT RI** **02840-001**

• In written correspondence, you may use abbreviations in the **street name.**

35 Main **St.** 1545 **Ave.** of the Americas

Do not abbreviate the name of a street used as part of a name.

59th Street Bridge

• In addresses, use two-letter postal abbreviations for **state or province names.**

Birmingham, **AL** Toronto, **ON**

For a complete list of postal abbreviations, see Figure 15.1 in chapter 15.

• In written correspondence, abbreviate words that stand for **city divisions.** If you use a period with these abbreviations, use only one, and precede them with a comma.

K Street, **NW.** 14th St., **SE.**

Always use the period when the directional word precedes a street name.

124 **E.** Drury Drive 14 **N.** 55th Ave.

Here are some abbreviations you may need to use.

Common Abbreviations of Place Names

AFB	Air Force Base
APO	American Post Office
Ave.	Avenue
Bldg.	Building
Blvd.	Boulevard
Ct.	Court
Dr.	Drive
E. or E	East
Hwy.	Highway
La.	Lane
Mt.	Mount
N. or N	North
NE. or NE	Northeast
NW. or NW	Northwest
Pkwy.	Parkway
Pl.	Place
P.O.	Post Office
Rd.	Road
R.F.D.	Rural Farm Delivery
RR.	Railroad
Rt. or Rte.	Route

Ry.	Railway
S. or S	South
SE. or SE	Southeast
Sq.	Square
St.	Street; Saint
Ste.	Saint
SW. or SW	Southwest
W. or W	West

Fig. 8.2

ORGANIZATIONS AND AGENCIES

Always spell, abbreviate, and punctuate the name of a company the way that company spells, abbreviates, and punctuates its name. When in doubt, check a reference source.

- Abbreviate **and** with an **ampersand (&)** if that is part of the company's legal name or customarily used abbreviation.

Standard **&** Poor's AT**&**T

- Abbreviate the words **incorporated** and **limited.**

General Foods, **Inc.** Wesley-Hart, **Ltd.**

Use a comma between the name and the abbreviation.

- In lists or citations, you may abbreviate the words **company, brothers,** and **corporation.**

Rodeway & **Co.** **Smith** Bros. Jenkins **Corp.**

Here are some abbreviations you may need to use. Notice that abbreviations of this sort in common use do not require periods.

Common Abbreviations of Organization and Agency Names

AA	Alcoholics Anonymous
AAA	American Automobile Association
ABA	American Bar Association; American Basketball Association; American Booksellers Association
ABC	American Broadcasting Company
ACLU	American Civil Liberties Union
AFL-CIO	American Federation of Labor and Congress of Industrial Organizations
AFT	American Federation of Teachers
AID	Agency for International Development
AMA	American Medical Association
AMEX	American Stock Exchange
ASPCA	American Society for the Prevention of Cruelty to Animals
AT&T	American Telephone and Telegraph
BIA	Bureau of Indian Affairs
BLM	Bureau of Land Management
CBS	Columbia Broadcasting System
CIA	Central Intelligence Agency
CNN	Cable News Network
EEC	European Economic Community
EEOC	Equal Employment Opportunity Commission
EPA	Environmental Protection Agency
FBI	Federal Bureau of Investigation
FDA	Food and Drug Administration
FHA	Federal Housing Administration
FRS	Federal Reserve System
GE	General Electric
GM	General Motors
GPO	Government Printing Office
IBM	International Business Machines
ILGWU	International Ladies' Garment Workers' Union

ILO	International Labor Organization
IMF	International Monetary Fund
INS	Immigration and Naturalization Service
IRS	Internal Revenue Service
ITT	International Telephone and Telegraph
MLA	Modern Language Association
MTV	Music Television
NAACP	National Association for the Advancement of Colored People
NBC	National Broadcasting Company
NCAA	National Collegiate Athletic Association
NEA	National Education Association; National Endowment for the Arts
NIH	National Institutes of Health
NLRB	National Labor Relations Board
NRC	Nuclear Regulatory Commission
NSC	National Security Council
NYSE	New York Stock Exchange
OAS	Organization of American States
OMB	Office of Management and Budget
PTA	Parent-Teachers' Association
RCA	Radio Corporation of America
SBA	Small Business Administration
TBS	Turner Broadcasting System
TVA	Tennessee Valley Authority
TWA	Trans World Airlines
UAW	United Automobile Workers
UFW	United Farmworkers
UN	United Nations
USCG	United States Coast Guard
USMA	United States Military Academy
USN	United States Navy
USO	United Service Organizations
VA	Veterans' Administration
VFW	Veterans of Foreign Wars

WHO	World Health Organization
YMCA/YWCA	Young Men's/Women's Christian Association
YMHA/YWHA	Young Men's/Women's Hebrew Association

Fig. 8.3

ACRONYMS

An acronym is an abbreviation formed from the first letter or letters in a phrase or a compound noun. Unlike a standard abbreviation, an acronym is pronounced as a word rather than as a series of letters.

standard abbreviation	**NBC** (N-B-C)
acronym	**NATO** (na.to)

Common Acronyms

ACTUP	AIDS Coalition to Unleash Power
AIDS	Auto-Immune Deficiency Syndrome
AWOL	Absent Without Official Leave
BASIC	Beginners All-purpose Symbolic Instruction Code
CARE	Cooperative for American Remittances to Everywhere
COBOL	Common Business Oriented Language
COLA	Cost-of-Living Adjustment
CORE	Congress of Racial Equality
FORTRAN	Formula Translation
HUD	Housing and Urban Development
laser	light amplification by stimulated emission of radiation
loran	long-range navigation

MADD	Mothers Against Drunk Driving
NASA	National Aeronautics and Space Administration
NATO	North Atlantic Treaty Organization
NOW	National Organization of Women
OPEC	Organization of Petroleum Exporting Countries
OSHA	Occupational Safety and Health Administration
PIN	personal identification number
radar	radio detecting and ranging
RAM	Random-Access Memory
REM	Rapid Eye Movement
ROM	Read-Only Memory
SADD	Students Against Drunk Driving
scuba	self-contained underwater breathing apparatus
sonar	sound, navigation, and ranging
SWAT	Special Weapons and Tactics
telex	teletypewriter exchange
UNESCO	United Nations Educational, Scientific, and Cultural Organization
UNICEF	United Nations Children's Fund
WAC	Women's Army Corps
WATS	Wide-Area Telecommunications Service
WAVES	Women Accepted for Volunteer Emergency Service
ZIP	Zone Improvement Plan

Fig. 8.4

CALENDAR DIVISIONS

In formal writing, spell out all dates. In lists, memos, or citations, you may abbreviate them.

Calendar Abbreviations

Months	Days
Jan.	Sun.
Feb.	Mon.
Mar.	Tues.
Apr.	Wed.
Aug.	Thurs.
Sept.	Fri.
Oct.	Sat.
Nov.	
Dec.	

Fig. 8.5

May, June, and *July* are never abbreviated.

TEXT CITATIONS

Abbreviations relating to parts of texts should only appear in a parenthetical reference or a citation. Here are some abbreviations you may need to use, especially when you are writing bibliographies or footnotes.

Common Abbreviations of Text-Related Words

app.	appendix
art.	article
c.	copyright
cf.	*confer* (compare)
ch.	chapter
col.	column

def.	definition
ed.	edition
e.g.	*exempli gratia* (for example)
et al.	*et alii* (and others)
etc.	*etcetera* (and so on)
fig.	figure
ibid.	*ibidem* (in the same place)
i.e.	*id est* (that is)
l.	line
ll.	lines
ms.	manuscript
no.	number
op.	opus
op. cit.	*opere citato* (in the work cited)
p.	page
pp.	pages
par.	paragraph
pl.	plate
pt.	part
pub.	publisher
q.v.	*quod vide* (which see)
sec.	section
v.	verse
vv.	verses
vol.	volume

Fig. 8.6

UNITS OF MEASURE

Never abbreviate measurements in text. You may choose to abbreviate them in tables and charts, citations and lists, and so on.

Your company stylebook may have specific rules governing

the use of periods in abbreviations of units of measure. Systems vary from place to place. For our purposes here, we will use a period with English (standard) units of measure and use no period with international and metric units. In scientific writing, periods are generally not used with units of measure, no matter what kind.

Common Abbreviations of Units of Measure

A	ampere
Å	angstrom
ac	alternating current
AM	amplitude modulation
at wt	atomic weight
avdp	avoirdupois
bbl	barrel
bd. ft.	board foot
bm	board measure
bp	boiling point
Btu	British thermal unit
bu	bushel
c or ct. or ¢	cent
°C	degree Celsius
cal	calorie
cc or cm^3	cubic centimeter
cd	candela
cL	centiliter
cm	centimeter
cm^2	square centimeter
cwt.	hundredweight
dc	direct current
dL	deciliter
dm	decimeter
doz.	dozen
dr.	dram

°F	degree Fahrenheit
fc	footcandle
fl. oz.	fluid ounce
FM	frequency modulation
ft.	foot
$ft.^2$	square foot
$ft.^3$	cubic foot
g	gram
gal.	gallon
gr.	grain
h. or hr.	hour
HF	high frequency
hg	hectogram
hL	hectoliter
hp	horsepower
Hz	hertz (cycles per second)
in.	inch
$in.^2$	square inch
$in.^3$	cubic inch
J	joule (kilogram-meter)
K	degree Kelvin
kg	kilogram
kL	kiloliter
km	kilometer
km/h	kilometers per hour
kn	knot (nautical mile per hour)
kW	kilowatt
L	liter
lb.	pound
LF	low frequency
m	meter
m^2	square meter
m^3	cubic meter
MHz	megahertz
mg	milligram

mi.	mile
$mi.^2$	square mile
µg	microgram
µm	micrometer
µs	microsecond
min.	minute
mL	milliliter
mm	millimeter
mo.	month
mol	mole
MPG	miles per gallon
MPH	miles per hour
ms	millisecond
ns	nanosecond
oz.	ounce
pct	percent
pk.	peck
pt.	pint
qt.	quart
R	roentgen
s	second; shilling
T	tesla; tablespoon; metric ton
tbsp.	tablespoon
tsp.	teaspoon
UHF	ultrahigh frequency
V	volt
VHF	very high frequency
W	watt
yd.	yard
$yd.^2$	square yard
$yd.^3$	cubic yard
yr.	year

Fig. 8.7

9

Numbers

Adding columns of figures or entering price codes may not appear in your job description, but sooner or later you will certainly have to deal with numbers in one form or another. In this chapter you will learn the basic rules that govern the writing of numbers.

USING WORDS

In ordinary text, spell out **numbers below 10** that do not indicate street addresses or units of time, measurement, or money.

Note that this style varies from place to place; check your company's stylebook.

nine folders
first example
five people
sixth grade

Exceptions are certain numbers that are customarily spelled out in general usage, such as parts of addresses, political divisions, or certain military units.

Twelve Oaks Farm
Ninety-third Congress
Third Reich
Ten Commandments
Eighth Ward
Fifth Battalion

• Spell out **numbers that begin sentences.**

Fifty years ago my father built this company.
Nineteen eighty-three was a banner year in sales.
Twenty-third in his Harvard class, he excelled everywhere.

If another number with a similar function follows three or fewer words later, spell out that number as well.

Fifty or **sixty** years ago, this was a different town.
Fifty years ago he arrived, and 10 years ago he retired.

• Spell out numbers under 100 that **precede a compound modifier** that contains a numeral.

fourteen 3-inch nails
thirty 8-pound bags

• Spell out most **fractions.**

One-third completed
three-tenths of the population

However, do not spell out mixed numbers.

8-½ truckloads
21-¼ pages long

SING FIGURES

In running text, use figures for **numbers 10 or above.**

14 copies   **33d** session   **187** votes

Vhen you write ordinal numbers ending in *3*, use the suffix *d* ather than *rd.*

incorrect	We attended the 123rd Ukrainian Festival.
correct	We attended the 123**d** Ukrainian Festival.

In ordinary text, if **two or more numbers** appear in a sen- ence, and one of them is **10 or greater,** use figures throughout.

The **25** chairs, **2** tables, and **4** desks are on back order.
The **5th** and **12th** boxes contain pencils.

Iowever, this applies only to numbers with the same function n the sentence (in this case, describing numbers of ordered tems). If numbers less than 10 appear that have a different unction, they may be spelled out.

We placed **two** orders for 25 chairs, 2 tables, and 4 desks.
The 5th and 12th boxes contain **eight** pencils each.

Use figures for most **street addresses.**

13 Dewer Place   **3** Sutton Place

Iowever, always spell out *One* in an address.

One Sutton Place

Use figures for **units of time, measurement, and money.**

9 years old	July **1776**	**£100**
0.5 meter long	**8-½** by **11** inches	**3**-month plan

This rule is always followed in technical or scientific writing. Your company may have specific rules that require using words for certain measurements. Check your stylebook.

- Use figures for **percents and proportions.**

15 percent	**90th** percentile	**1** to **2**

Use the word *percent* in most ordinary text. In statistical or scientific documents, use the symbol %.

FIGURES ABOVE 1,000

- Use **commas** to set off groups of three digits.

1,000,000	**5,401**	**20,000**

FIGURES ABOVE 1,000,000

- Use the word *million* or *billion* where it may improve comprehension, especially in writing amounts of money.

$15 **million** ***[instead of $15,000,000]***	10 **billion**	2.75 **million**

Remember that Americans use *billion* to mean 1,000 million. In Great Britain, *billion* means 1 million million.

DATES

- Use figures to write **most dates.**

14 August **1945**	June **4, 1902**

• Spell out **centuries and decades.**

the **sixteenth** century   the gay **nineties**

However, use figures if the century is included with the decade.

the **1990's**   during the **1940's**

• To designate specific eras before or after the year 1, use the initials B.C. (before Christ) or A.D. (*anno Domini*). These initials are customarily written in small capitals.

second century **B.C.**   **A.D.** 281

Notice that **A.D.** precedes the number reference, but **B.C.** follows it.

• Do not use informal usage in formal writing.

incorrect	We last met on 3/12/92.
correct	We last met on **March 12, 1992.**
	We last met on **12 March 1992.**

One of the problems with informal usage is that it can be misinterpreted. To someone from Great Britain, 3/12/92 means December 3, 1992.

ROMAN NUMERALS

In the Roman system, a repeated letter repeats its value; a letter placed before one of greater value subtracts from it; a letter placed after one of greater value adds to it; and a dash over a letter means the value is multiplied by 1,000.

• Capitalize roman numerals used in **dates, outlines, divisions of plays, musical notation,** or **proper names.**

Act **II**   John Jacob **III**

• Lowercase roman numerals used to page **front or back matter** in a document or book.

The preface begins on page **vii.**

Roman Numerals

I	1	XXV	25	CL	150
II	2	XXIX	29	CC	200
III	3	XXX	30	CCC	300
IV	4	XXI	31	CD	400
V	5	XXV	35	D	500
VI	6	XL	40	DC	600
VII	7	L	50	DCC	700
VIII	8	LV	55	DCCC	800
IX	9	LX	60	CM	900
X	10	LXV	65	M	1,000
XI	11	LXIX	69	MD	1,500
XV	15	LXX	70	MM	2,000
XIX	19	LXXX	80	MV	4,000
XX	20	XC	90	V	5,000
XXI	21	C	100	M	1,000,000

Fig. 9.1

MATHEMATICS

• Use **underlining or italics** to indicate **mathematical terms.**

$\frac{1}{2}\underline{x} = 5$ $\qquad$ $r = d/t$

• When displaying columns of figures, **align ones, tens, hundreds,** and so on.

123	**$10.45**	**14**
321.54	**2.10**	**+ 210**
4,120.3	**16.55**	**224**

- When displaying equations, **align equal signs.**

We know that

$$
\begin{aligned}
& 11 + 3 = 14 \\
\text{and} \quad & 14 - 11 = 3
\end{aligned}
$$

- Use **parentheses, brackets, and braces** in that order from inside to outside in complex equations.

$$x = \{2[4y - (3 + y)]\}$$

Common Mathematical Signs and Symbols

$=$	equal to	$\surd$	square root sign
$+$	plus	^{2}	squared
$-$	minus	π	*pi* (3.1416)
$\times$	times	∞	infinity
$\div$	divided by	Σ	algebraic sum
$\pm$	plus or minus	δ	variation of
$\approx$	approximately equal to	$!$	factorial
$\equiv$	identical to	$\in$	is an element of
$\cong$	congruent to	$^\circ$	degree
$\perp$	perpendicular to	$'$	prime; minute
$\parallel$	parallel to	$''$	double prime; second
$<$	less than	$:$	ratio
$>$	greater than	$::$	proportion
$\leq$	less than or equal to	$\cup$	union with
$\geq$	greater than or equal to	$\cap$	intersection with
$\neq$	not equal to	$\varnothing$	null set

Fig. 9.2

UNITS OF MEASURE

Be consistent in dealing with units of measure. Do not switch from metric to standard measurement indiscriminately.

incorrect **We drove 50 miles; they only went 14 kilometers.**
correct **We drove 50 miles; they only went 22.5 miles.**
We drove 31 kilometers; they only went 14 kilometers.

Once you choose your system of measurement, you may always include the other system's measures abbreviated in parentheses.

We drove 50 miles (31 km); they only went 22.5 miles (14 km).

Conversion Tables of Weights and Measures

Length

1 kilometer	=	0.62137 mile				
1 meter	=	39.37 inches	=	3.28 feet	=	1.1 yard
1 centimeter	=	0.3937 inch				
1 millimeter	=	0.0394 inch				
1 mile	=	1.6093 kilometers				
1 yard	=	0.9144 meter				
1 foot	=	0.3048 meter				
1 inch	=	2.54 centimeters				

Area

1 hectare	=	10,000 square meters	=	2.471 acres
1 acre	=	0.4047 hectare		

Weight

1 kilogram	=	2.2046 pounds
1 hectogram	=	3.5274 ounces
1 gram	=	15.432 grains
1 pound	=	0.4536 kilogram
1 ounce	=	28.35 grams
1 grain	=	0.0648 grams

Capacity

1 hectoliter	=	2.838 bushels	=	26.417 gallons
1 dekaliter	=	1.135 pecks	=	2.6417 gallons
1 liter	=	0.908 dry quart	=	1.0567 quarts
1 centiliter	=	0.6102 cubic inch	=	0.338 fluid ounce
1 bushel	=	35.24 liters		
1 peck	=	8.810 liters		
1 dry quart	=	1.101 liters		
1 cubic inch	=	16.39 cubic centimeters		
1 gallon	=	3.785 liters		
1 quart	=	0.9463 liters		

Fig. 9.3

10

Letters

- Parts of Letters
- Letter Styles
- Multiple-Page Letters
- Envelopes

A large part of your written communication on the job will be in the form of business letters. Business letters may be written for a variety of reasons: to acknowledge receipt, to show appreciation, to make inquiries, to place orders, to request payments, and so on. Although there are several different styles of business letters, there are standardized rules for their composition. Having standardized versions (or templates) saved on your computer can help you remain consistent and efficient.

PARTS OF LETTERS

All business letters must contain these parts:

- date
- inside address
- body
- signature

Most business letters also contain the following:

- salutation
- closing
- initials of typist

Some business letters contain these parts as well:

- delivery notation
- attention line
- subject
- enclosure or copy notations

The example that follows contains every one of these parts. You can see at a glance where each one belongs.

Annotated Business Letter

1 **STANDARD PRODUCTIONS**
21 Union Street
Brooklyn, NY 11215
(718) 555-1200

← 2 lines

2 19 July, 1995

3 EXPRESS MAIL } ← 3 to 10 lines

4 Attention: Ms. Grace Lefevre
5 Tokay Manufacturing Co.
1222 Delta Rd.
Homer, NY 13077

← 2 lines

6 Dear Ms. Lefevre:

← 2 lines

7 Re: Industrial Age Convention

← 2 lines

8 We would like very much to secure a booth for your convention in upstate New York the week of October 15. We will need tables and chairs, but we will supply shelving.

← 2 lines

Attached is our check in the amount of $400 to secure a booth in row A. If you have any questions, please call.

← 2 lines

9 Very truly yours,

← 4 lines

10 Charles Bloch
Assistant Manager

← 2 lines

11 CB/le
12 Enclosure

Fig. 10.1

1. Letterhead

Most businesses have their own letterhead stationery on which all business letters are typed. Most letterheads include the company name, street address, city, state, and ZIP code. This eliminates the need to type a return address on the letter.

2. Date

Space the date at least two lines below the letterhead on your stationery. Do not use abbreviations in the date. You may use either of these styles:

July 19, 1995 **19 July 1995**

3. Delivery Notation

Delivery notations may be written in capital letters halfway between the date and the attention line or inside address. Such notations may include any of the following:

AIR MAIL	BY MESSENGER	CERTIFIED MAIL
CONFIDENTIAL	EYES ONLY	HOLD FOR ARRIVAL
PERSONAL	REGISTERED MAIL	SPECIAL DELIVERY

4. Attention Line

The attention line or first line of the inside address appears at least three lines below the date—up to ten lines below the date in a short letter. You may send a letter to an individual, in which case his or her name becomes part of the inside address. You may, however, send a letter to the attention of someone at a company with the emphasis on the company rather than the individual. In this case, use the word *Attention* to alert mailroom or office personnel to the name of the correct recipient. You may or may not include a colon after the word *Attention.*

5. Inside Address

This may include the name of an individual. It always includes the company name, street address, city, state, and ZIP code. The company name should be written just as it appears on any correspondence from that company, including abbreviations or ampersands (&). (See Chapter 15 for more information on writing addresses correctly.)

6. Salutation

Some letter styles forgo this courtesy. (See Figure 10.7.) Most often, however, you will include the name of the person to whom the letter is addressed, preceded by *Dear* and followed by a colon. (In the style known as "open punctuation," no colon is used after the salutation, and no comma is used after the closing.) Do not use first names unless you know the person very well. Do not use the person's job title here unless the addressee is a member of the Armed Forces or a politician.

formal	**Dear Mr. Lopez:**	**Dear Messrs. Lopez:**
informal	**Dear Ricardo:**	**Dear Ricardo and Carlos:**
incorrect	**Dear Art Director Lopez:**	

On occasion, you will have to send a letter without knowing the name of the person who will receive it. You may use a salutation such as one of these.

To Whom It May Concern: **Dear Planning Committee:**

Alternatively, you may choose a letter style that avoids use of a salutation. (See Figure 10.7 for an example.)

Certain people in high offices require specific forms of address. Here are examples of forms you may need to use.

Forms of Address

Title	Inside Address	Salutation
Ambassador (U.S.)	The Honorable (name)	Sir:/Madam:
Ambassador (other)	His/Her Excellency, (name)	Excellency:
Archbishop	The Most Reverend (name)	Your Excellency:
Associate Justice	The Honorable (name)	Dear Justice (surname):
Attorney General	The Honorable (name)	Sir:/Madam:
Bishop (Methodist)	Bishop (name)	Dear Bishop (surname):
Bishop (Episcopal)	The Right Reverend (name)	Right Reverend Sir:
Bishop (Roman Catholic)	The Most Reverend (name)	Most Reverend Sir:
Cabinet Official	The Honorable (name)	Sir:/Madam:
Cardinal	His Eminence (first name) Cardinal (surname)	Your Eminence:
Chief Justice	The Chief Justice	Dear Mr./Madam Chief Justice:
Clergy (Protestant)	The Reverend (name)	Dear Reverend (surname):
Governor	The Honorable (name)	Dear Governor (surname):
Judge	The Honorable (name)	Dear Judge (surname):
Lawyer	(name), Esq.	Dear Mr./Ms. (surname):
Mayor	His/Her Honor, The Mayor	Dear Mayor (surname):
Pope	His Holiness the Pope	Your Holiness:
President	The President	Dear Mr./Ms. President:
Priest (Roman Catholic)	The Reverend (name)	Reverend Father:

Prime Minister	His/Her Excellency, (name)	Excellency:
Professor	Professor/Dr. (name)	Dear Professor/Dr. (surname)
Rabbi	Rabbi (name)	Dear Rabbi (surname):
Representative	The Honorable (name)	Sir:/Madam:
Senator	The Honorable (name)	Sir:/Madam:
U.N. Secretary-General	His Excellency (name)	Your Excellency:

Fig. 10.2

When you write less formally, you may often address even high-ranking persons with less formal salutations. For example, members of the House of Representatives may be addressed "Dear Mr./Ms.," and senators may be addressed "Dear Senator (name)."

7. Subject

If your addressee receives a lot of mail each day, a subject line, while it is not required, may help her or him classify your letter without having to read the whole thing. You may use one of these styles.

Re: Five-Year Plan **Subject: Five-Year Plan**

8. Body

This is the meat of the letter. In the body, you make your request, give your information, and so on. The body is usually single spaced with double spaces between paragraphs. The key to writing a good letter is to make it short and to the point.

Use formal language in the body of a business letter. Avoid slang, abbreviations, and contractions. Use language that is inoffensive, even in a complaint letter.

Inoffensive language also means language that is gender-neutral. Some words have gender-specific meanings; those words should be used in pairs to indicate that either might be appropriate: *his* or *hers, fraternity* or *sorority, mistress* or *master.* Other traditional words can be replaced. Here is a list that may prove useful:

Non-Sexist Terminology

instead of **anchorman**	use **news anchor**
instead of **businesswoman**	use **businessperson**
instead of **cleaning woman**	use **housecleaner**
instead of **congressman**	use **representative**
instead of **fireman**	use **fire fighter**
instead of **forefathers**	use **ancestors**
instead of **housewife**	use **homemaker**
instead of **mailman**	use **mail carrier**
instead of **mankind**	use **humankind, humanity**
instead of **manned**	use **staffed**
instead of **manpower**	use **workforce**
instead of **meter maid**	use **traffic officer**
instead of **policeman**	use **police officer**
instead of **saleswoman**	use **salesperson**
instead of **stewardess**	use **flight attendant**
instead of **weatherman**	use **meteorologist**
instead of **workman**	use **worker**

Fig. 10.3

9. Closing

Type the closing two lines below the final line of the body. Capitalize the first word and follow the closing with a comma. (If you are using open punctuation, and have used no colon after the salutation, omit the comma here.)

formal	**Very truly yours,**	**Yours truly,**	**Respectfully,**
less formal	**Sincerely,**	**Cordially,**	
informal	**Regards,**	**Best wishes,**	**Yours,**

10. Signature

The name of the writer (as opposed to that of the typist) appears four lines below the closing to make room for the writer to sign. If the job title is included, it appears one line below that.

Very truly yours,

Chas Bloch

Charles Bloch
Assistant Manager

Sincerely,

Laura Elsen

Laura Elsen
Assistant to Mr. Bloch

Yours truly,

Julie Eng

Julie Eng, M.D.

Respectfully,

John Friend EG

John Friend, Provost
[signed by an assistant; his initials follow the signature]

You may include the name of your company two lines below the closing.

Very truly yours,

STANDARD PRODUCTIONS

Chas Bloch

Charles Bloch
Assistant Manager

11. Initials of Typist

These initials appear two lines below the signature. The typist's initials appear in lowercase letters without periods. If the letter-signer's initials are included, they appear in capital letters preceding the typist's initials.

le	**CB/le or CB:le**

12. Enclosure or Copy Notations

If you are including something along with the letter, or you have sent more than one copy of the letter, you may alert the sender here, one line below the initials of the typist. Some sample notations appear below.

multiple enclosures	**Enclosures—Tapes**	**or**	**Enclosures 3**
copy sent	**cc: David Haring**	**or**	**c David Haring**
blind copy sent	**bc: David Haring**	**or**	**bc David Haring**

When you do not want the recipient to know that a copy of the letter has been sent elsewhere, you call the copy you send a "blind copy." The notation *bc* appears *only* on your office copy and on the second recipient's copy. Do not make a mistake and write *bc* on the original.

LETTER STYLES

Today, nearly all business letters are typed in block style, without paragraph indentations. Letters should be framed by margins of white space. Generally, a letter of 100 words or less should have a line width from left to right of around four inches, a letter of around 100–200 words should have a line width of five inches, and a letter of 200 words or more should have a line width of six inches. How you set your margins will depend on the size of your type and on whether you are using a typewriter or a word processor.

There are four main styles of business letters: block, modified block, paragraphed, and simplified block. Your company stylebook may recommend one style. Otherwise, choose the one that works best for your purposes, and be consistent in its use. If you send out a great number of similar letters, it is easy to create a sample format, or template, on your computer and use it as a guide every time you write a letter.

Block Letter of Acknowledgment

KMAC Radio
195 Cedar Avenue
Fresno, CA 93703

3 October 1994

All lines are flush with the left margin.

Mr. Daniel Cameron
Communications, Ltd.
541 Connecticut Ave., NW
Washington, DC 20015

Dear Mr. Cameron:

We received the brochure we requested on "Marketing Strategies for Small Media" on October 1 and greatly appreciate your quick response. In answer to your question, we have been working in the Country and Western format since 1991.

I enclose a sample playlist for your files. Thank you again for your information.

Sincerely,

KMAC

Martha Weinstock

Ms. Martha Weinstock
Vice President

MW/az
Enclosure

Fig. 10.4

Modified Block Letter of Appreciation

Allan Marcus, CPA
62 Burnett Avenue
San Francisco, CA 94131

12 June 1995

All lines are flush with the left margin, with the exception of the date, closing, and signature, which are vertically aligned right of center.

Ms. Alicia Andrews
San Francisco Bureau of Trade
16 Office Tower
14–43 Burnett Avenue
San Francisco, CA 94131

Dear Ms. Andrews:

It was so kind of you to include me in your plans for "San Francisco Small Business Days." I truly enjoyed working with you and Ms. Matthews, and I was overwhelmed to receive your nomination for "Small Business of the Year."

Let me commend you on a successful celebration of small businesses in our city. Thank you again for your support.

Yours truly,

Allan Marcus

Allan Marcus, CPA

db
cc: Caroline Matthews

Fig. 10.5

Paragraphed Letter Placing an Order

Delacourt Jewelers
178 Creek Drive
Cincinnati, OH 45241
(513) 555-1818

1 May 1994

This sets up like a modified block letter (Figure 10.5), but paragraphs are indented.

Attention: Sales Division
Soares Handmade Products
190 Elm St.
Waterbury, VT 05676

Dear Sales Representative:

We would like to order the following items from your spring catalog:

Catalog No.	Item	Quantity	Unit Price	Total
154-K	silver ankh	25	$4	$100.00
167-P	turquoise star	15	$5	$75.00
				$175.00
			tax, shipping, and handling	13.75
				$188.75

Enclosed please find our check in the amount of $188.75. You may ship these items to the address on our letterhead. We understand that they will be shipped no later than May 5.

Sincerely,

G. Roche

Gloria Roche, Retail Manager

GR/fe
Enclosure—Check

Fig. 10.6

Simplified Block Letter Requesting Payment

Northside Chiropractic
218 First Avenue
Seattle, WA 98121
(206) 555-0222

24 February 1995

The "simplified" letter has no salutation or closing. All lines are flush left.

Ms. Rachelle Phillips
2703 34th Ave. S.
Seattle, WA 98144

RE: PATIENT FILE 481-04

Payment has not yet been received for your treatments of November 12, 15, and 29. We remind you that patients are responsible for payments for procedures not covered by their insurance policies.

Attached are copies of your bills. Please call as soon as possible to arrange a schedule for payment.

I look forward to hearing from you.

Kelsey Kwong
Kelsey Kwong, Manager
Billing Department

nc
Enclosure

Fig. 10.7

MULTIPLE-PAGE LETTERS

Type the first page of a business letter on letterhead stationery. Type all additional pages on plain paper of the same color, weight, and size. Use the same left and right margins as on page 1, but include a heading at the top of each page from page 2 on. The heading should include the name of the letter's recipient, the page number, and the date.

horizontal style

Ms. Grace Lefevre 2 19 July, 1995

block style

Ms. Grace Lefevre
Page 2
July 19, 1995

Leave three spaces below the heading and continue with the body of the letter. Never break a page at a hyphen or after the first line of a paragraph. Always include at least two lines of the body on the last page, preceding the closing and signature.

ENVELOPES

The United States Postal Service has specific recommendations governing the addressing of envelopes. Whether you choose to follow all of them depends on the guidelines in your company stylebook. Keep in mind that the Post Office has developed its recommendations in order to speed sorting and service, so complying with them can only enhance your written communication.

Annotated No. 10 Envelope

Fig. 10.8

1. Return Address

Usually, letterhead stationery comes with envelopes that contain a preprinted return address. This should appear on the front of the envelope.

2. Post Office Delivery Notation

Notations appear in capital letters two lines below the stamp. Post office delivery notations may include these:

AIR MAIL	**CERTIFIED MAIL**
REGISTERED MAIL	**SPECIAL DELIVERY**

3. In-House Delivery Notations

Notations that tell what should become of a letter once it reaches its destination appear three lines below the return address. Important words are capitalized, and the notation is underlined. Notations of this kind include these:

Confidential ***Eyes Only*** ***Personal***

4. Delivery Address

Postal Service guidelines suggest that all lines in a typed address be typed single space, aligned on the left, and capitalized. Eliminate all punctuation marks except for hyphens in numbers, and limit the address to six lines at most.

5. Attention Line or Addressee

It is easiest to include the attention line right where the addressee's name would go. You should usually include a title: *DR, MR, MS,* and so on.

6. Company Name

If there is a company name, this is where it belongs. As you did on the inside address, follow the company's own spelling and punctuation conventions when you write its name.

7. Street Address

Include any room, apartment, or suite number on the same line as the street address, as long as it will fit. If it will not fit, put that information on the line above the street address. Use standard abbreviations for roads, streets, and so on. (See Figure 8.2.)

8. City, State, and Zip Code

Once again, the Postal Service does not require standard punctuation here. If possible, use the ZIP + 4 code; this helps postal workers zero in on the exact location of your addressee. You must use standard postal abbreviations of state names. (See Figure 15.1 for a complete list.) If you are sending a letter to a foreign country, type the country name one line below the name of the city. Be sure to include any relevant codes; check the return address on any correspondence the addressee has sent to you.

11

Memos

- Parts of Memos
- Memo Styles

Memos, or memoranda, are short written notes dispatched among members of the same company. Often memos stay within a single office building and are transmitted *via* interoffice mail. Sometimes memos are sent to branch offices in other buildings or cities.

PARTS OF MEMOS

Most memos contain these parts, which may appear in one of several orders:

- date
- to
- from
- subject

They may also contain:

- initials of typist
- enclosure or copy notations

The memo that follows shows one possible arrangement of these parts.

Annotated Memo

		← 10 lines from top
1 DATE:	14 June, 1994	***double space between each line in the heading***
2 TO:	Sandra Fink, Human Resources	
3 FROM:	Rick Delaware, Benefits	
4 SUBJECT:	Medical Forms	
		← 3 lines
5	Please note that any new personnel are expected to complete the attached forms within six weeks of employment. If you have any questions, please call me at extension 3740.	
		← 2 lines
6	RD/de	
7	Enclosures	
8	cc: Jasper Hill Mara Prahbu Sonya Wright	

Fig. 11.1

1. Date

It is always clearest to type the date out completely, using either of these styles:

June 14, 1994 **14 June 1994**

The date may appear before or after the TO/FROM notations.

2. To

Your company style may require you to tell whom the memo is FROM *before* you tell whom it is TO. Most TO references contain both a name and a job title or department. You need not include titles such as *Mr.* or *Ms.*

Your TO section may contain more than one name. If so, it should list the names of the recipients alphabetically or in order of rank in your company's chain of command.

3. From

This should list the sender's name and title or department. There is no formal signature on a memo, but the sender may choose to initial or sign to the right of the FROM line or below the body of the memo.

4. Subject

This should be clear and concise. People receive many memos during the week, and they need to be able to sort through them quickly and file them accurately.

5. Body

Type the body single spaced in block style. Double space between paragraphs. The goal is precision and ease of reading, so use numbered or otherwise highlighted points if they can make your memo clearer.

6. Initials of Typist

These initials appear two lines below the body. The typist's initials appear in lowercase letters without periods. If the memo-sender's initials are included, they appear in capital letters preceding the typist's initials.

de **RD/de** **or** **RD:de**

7. Enclosure Notation

If you are including something along with the memo, you may alert the sender here, one or two lines below the initials of the typist. You may wish to tell exactly what is being enclosed.

Enclosures—Medical Forms

8. Copy Notation

If you do not list every recipient's name in the TO section, you may use a copy notation to indicate the memo's circulation. Again, list people's names alphabetically or according to rank.

MEMO STYLES

Your company may have preprinted memo forms, or you may need to create such a form with a macro on your computer. Short memos may be written on 8½- × 5½-inch paper—half a sheet of regular bond. Begin the memo 10 lines from the top of the page. If letterhead is used, begin at least two lines below the letterhead.

The memo's body may align with the leftmost typed element in the heading or with the *S* in *SUBJECT*. Here are examples of correct memo styles. If your company does not specify a style, choose one, but be consistent in its use.

Preprinted Memo Form

TO: Stan Jenkins, Paul Mars, Doris Milltown, Art Snow
FROM: Jennifer Kenyon, Production Manager
DATE: September 5, 1995
SUBJECT: *Test Your Child's Intelligence,* tk 1996

The abovementioned title will reach the copyediting department on September 15. All artwork must be submitted to editorial for approval no later than October 1. This title takes priority over *Eyes Only* and *Standing Room.* Please adjust your schedules accordingly.

Thanks.

fw

Fig. 11.2

Letterhead Memo

WHISTLER, LEROY & SANDLER
Attorneys-at-Law
28-85 Parkinson Way
Tampa, FL 33631-3123
(813) 555-1313

TO All Associates
FROM Sarah Weeks, Office Manager
DATE November 1, 1996
SUBJECT Recycling

It has come to my attention that a number of the associates fail to use the paper recycling bins located in the rear of the copying room. We generate hundreds of pounds of paper each week; let's try to comply with Tampa's recycling regulations.

Fig. 11.3

Plain-Paper Memo

14 March 1996

TO: Sydney Becu, Director of Sales
FROM: Gina Lopinto, Consultant, Northeast Region
SUBJECT: In-service Dates

I will be on the road doing in-services on the following dates.

1. March 19—East Barre Junior High School, Barre, VT
2. March 30—Franklin Middle School, Nashua, NH
3. April 13–14—Dryden High School, Dryden, NY
4. April 19—Binghamton Board of Education, Binghamton, NY

I will call in every other day as usual.

GL:rn
Enclosure—In-service Agenda
c Derek Marston, Marketing

Fig. 11.4

12

Reports

- Parts of Reports
- Tables and Graphs
- Footnotes and Endnotes
- Bibliographies and Reference Notes

Reports may contain information about inventory, recommendations for research and development, results of investigations, analyses of merchandise, evaluations of job performance, requests for grants, and so on. Public companies regularly prepare annual reports for stockholders that detail the workings of the company and its profits and losses. The goals of most reports are to present facts, draw conclusions, and make recommendations.

PARTS OF REPORTS

Depending on its size, a report may contain all or some of these parts:

- letter of transmittal
- title page
- table of contents

- list of figures
- abstract or executive summary
- body
- references or bibliography
- appendix or appendices
- index

1. Letter of Transmittal

This may be a cover letter, or it may be part of the report, in which case it usually follows the title page. The purpose of the letter of transmittal is to introduce the report to the reader.

2. Title Page

This lists the title of the report, the author or authors of the report, the name and address of the company issuing the report, and the date the report was issued. The elements of the title page should be centered vertically and horizontally on the page.

3. Table of Contents

The table of contents lists the main sections of the report and the page number on which each section begins. A very long report may be broken into chapters, in which case the table of contents will list the chapter titles. Otherwise, the table of contents will list major headings and occasionally subheadings as well. Tables of contents may use outline form, with roman numerals denoting major headings, or they may be set up as in Figure 12.3. Leaders (. . .) are usually used to connect each heading to its page reference.

Notice that the page numbers of any introductory material are listed as lowercase roman numerals, and the first page of the body of the report begins on page 1 (in arabic numerals).

4. List of Figures

Reports may contain figures such as tables, charts, graphs, and illustrations. It may help your reader sort through this information if you list figures in order of appearance in their own separate table of contents. List the title of each figure with its corresponding page number. If the figures are numbered in the text, list the numbers as well.

5. Abstract or Executive Summary

A long report may benefit from the inclusion of a summary that ranges from one to three pages and lists the main topics to be covered in the report. A good abstract outlines the main features of the report; for example, the problem and suggested solution; or the objective, facts, conclusions, and recommendations. It does not go into detail; that is left to the body of the report.

6. Body

The body of any report begins with an introduction. Facts are given, conclusions are drawn, and recommendations, if any, are made. The body may be divided into chapters, each of which has a title and begins on a new page. It can also be divided into sections, each of which has a heading. There are three main styles of headings.

centered head

OUR NEW HEALTH PLAN

or **Our New Health Plan**

The text follows flush left, two lines below the heading.

flush left head

OUR NEW HEALTH PLAN **or**
Our New Health Plan

The text follows flush left, two lines below the heading.

running head

Our New Health Plan **or**

Our New Health Plan The text runs in on the same line as the heading.

If you have subheadings in your report, use the first style of heading for main headings and the second for subheadings, or use the second style for main headings and the third for subheadings. If you need a sub-subheading, use the first style for main headings, the second for subheadings, and the third for sub-subheadings.

7. References or Bibliography

A reference list may give the names of works recommended by the authors of the report for further information. It may list these works under headings that define the type of work mentioned or the topic of the work.

A bibliography is a list of those works cited in or used to write the report. Bibliographic style is discussed on pages 188–189.

8. Appendix or Appendices

An appendix or appendices may follow the bibliography. These pages contain materials that support the report but do not necessarily belong in the body. Statistical references, extensive graphs and tables, maps, surveys, questionnaires, and sketches may be among the materials included as appendices.

9. Index

A very long report may have an index. This is an alphabetized list of the report's topics together with the page numbers on which those topics are found. The index allows for more detail than the table of contents; it lists *every* page reference for a given topic, not just the first page on which a main heading appears.

The figures that follow show a sample letter of transmittal, a sample title page, a sample table of contents, a sample list of figures, and a sample abstract.

Letter of Transmittal

14 April 1995

Mr. Hector Alvarez
Boyco Construction
984 Peachdale Ave.
Memphis, TN 38101

RESULTS OF WATER TESTS ON THREE BUILDING SITES

Attached is the report that you requested, showing the results of water tests on three building sites outside the Memphis city limits. The report reviews our findings, and the appendices show the exact results of coliform and other tests.

We looked at three sites: Bendix Drive near the Bendix Mall, Alcourt Place, and the dead end road labeled "K" off Route 5. Maps in the appendix show the exact locations of the tests.

I hope that you find this report comprehensive enough for your needs. If you have any questions, please call me.

Barbara Felch, Director
Redwing Diagnostic Laboratory

Fig. 12.1

Title Page

RESULTS OF WATER TESTS ON THREE BUILDING SITES

Barbara Felch & Associates
April, 1995

Redwing Diagnostic Laboratories
Memphis, Tennessee

Fig. 12.2

Table of Contents

CONTENTS

ii

Fig. 12.3

List of Figures

FIGURES

iii

Fig. 12.4

Abstract

ABSTRACT

Redwing Diagnostic Laboratory tested three building sites, hereafter denoted as A, B, and C, to measure their water potability against specifications of the Public Drinking Water of Tennessee Sanitary Code. Standard tests were used to test for coliform, chlorine, and three other factors.

Results were negative for Sites A and B, but Site C showed evidence of *E. coli* infestation in excess of the count acceptable to the state of Tennessee.

We recommend that building begin on Sites A and B, but Site C will require cleaning up to remove contamination from farms upstream. We have included approximate costs of such clean up.

iv

Fig. 12.5

TABLES AND GRAPHS

Tables give statistical information in rows and columns. Center the title of the table or type it flush left, and be consistent—set up all tables the same way. There should be equal space between the columns of a table. Many word processing programs help you here by including a "column" mode that spaces columns automatically. The table should not break between pages. If it is very large, type it and reduce it, type it in a smaller typeface than the body of the text, or extend it over a spread of pages so that the table takes up both the left- and right-hand page.

You may label your table with a number, calling it Table 1 or Figure 1. If the table appears in Appendix A, call it Table A-1 or Figure A-1. If it appears in Appendix B, call it Table B-1 or Figure B-1, and so on.

Remember that your goal is to make data logical and easy to read. Use spacing, boldfacing, different type sizes, and other graphic aids to improve your table's readability.

Table

Figure 7
Requirements to Bring Site C Up to Code

Improvement	*Time Frame*	*Approximate Cost*
Clean up *E. coli*	April–August	$11,500
Add iron filters	May	$ 500
Drill new well	August	$ 8,000
Run new tests	September	$ 750
		$20,750 total

Fig. 12.6

Graphs, like tables, are designed to display statistical information. The most common graphs are line graphs, bar graphs, and circle graphs. You may send statistics out to a specialist to have graphs rendered, or you may be able to use your own software to design and format a graph.

Line graphs and bar graphs have two axes, vertical and horizontal. The axes may be labeled in any number of ways. If one axis shows numbers, it is generally best to begin at zero and increase by equal increments. Use a bar graph to make direct comparisons. Use a line graph to show change. Here are examples of each.

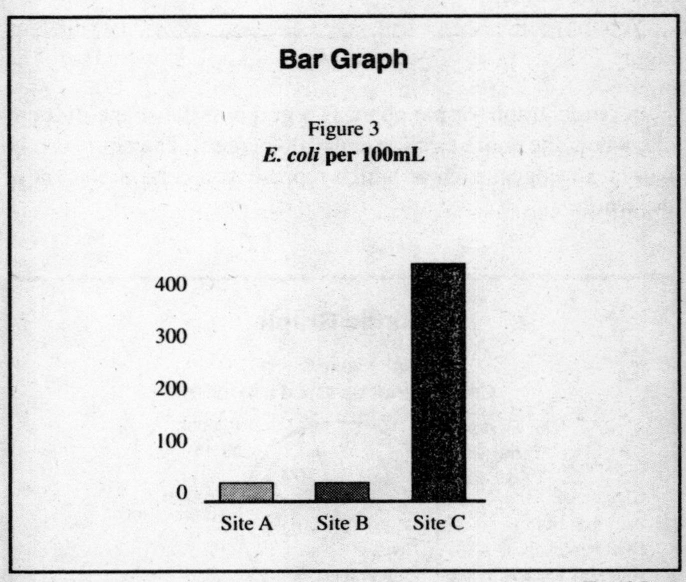

Fig. 12.7

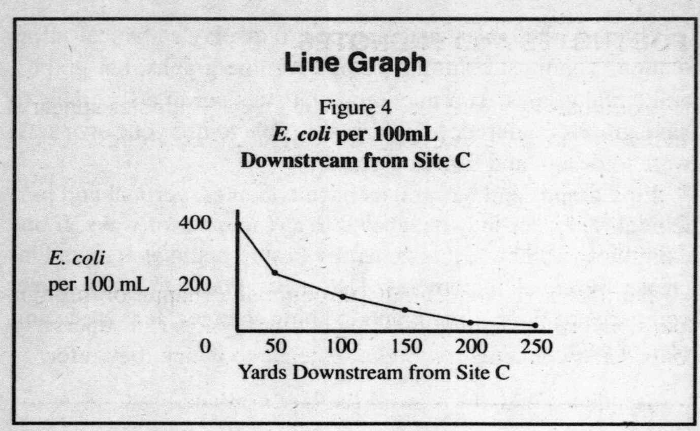

Fig. 12.8

A circle graph, or pie chart, is a graph in the shape of a circle, where the entire circle equals 100 percent. The circle is broken into wedges, each of which represents a certain percent of the whole.

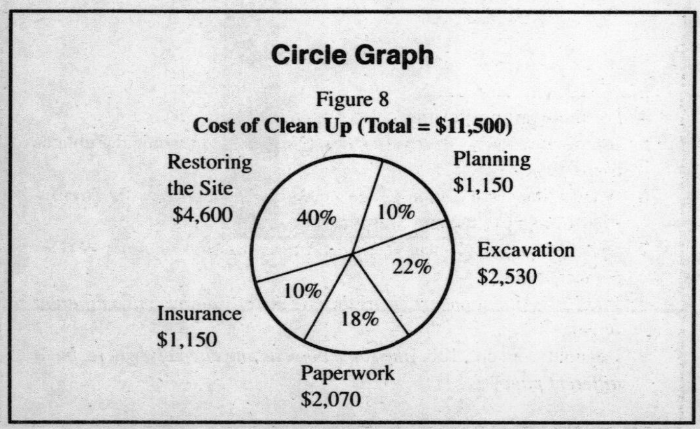

Fig. 12.9

FOOTNOTES AND ENDNOTES

Footnotes appear at the bottom of a page. Endnotes appear at the end of a report. Use notes to designate these things:

- references to sources
- direct quotations
- author's asides

Number notes sequentially throughout a chapter or throughout a report. In running text, the numbers appear in superscript outside any punctuation in the sentence to which they refer.

It appears that Site A meets the specifications.[4]

As you type, keep track of the number of footnotes on a page and leave room at the bottom of the page to accommodate them. After your last line of text, hit the return key and type a horizontal underline about two inches long one line below that line of text. Skip a space, and begin your footnotes. It is easiest to number footnotes on the line flush left. Reducing their type size helps differentiate them from the text.

Footnotes

---

4. For more on specifications, see Appendix A.
5. Joseph Reynolds, *Water Analysis* (New York: Technical Publications, 1987), 123–125.
6. Wendy Marx and Simon Grenville, *Data Crunching in the Twenty-First Century* (Chicago: Sunshine Press, 1992), 47.
7. Sarita Marah, "Coliform Testing," *Journal of Microbiology* 19 (December, 1993): 244–45.
8. Ibid., 247. [*the same article as the one directly above, but a different page*]
9. Reynolds, op. cit., 130. [*the same book as one cited elsewhere, but a different page*]

Fig. 12.10

Endnotes are often more convenient than footnotes. You need not estimate numbers of lines of text in order to fit endnotes, since they are grouped together on a page or pages at the end of the report. Endnotes may also be very long, which may be appropriate if you need to include explanatory remarks by the author. If you include endnotes instead of footnotes, place them after the appendix and before the bibliography. Head a single page of endnotes with the word "Notes." If there are multiple pages of endnotes, head the pages with descriptive headings such as "Notes to Pages 1–5," "Notes to Pages 6–14," and so on.

Many word processing programs now offer a footnoting function, which automatically allows enough space at the bottom of the page, keeps the notes numbered sequentially, and so on. For very complicated work, for example academic articles, there is software available specifically for footnotes and endnotes.

BIBLIOGRAPHIES AND REFERENCE NOTES

A bibliography lists the references used in compiling the report. List references in alphabetical order by authors' last names. You may list books and periodicals separately. Type the authors' names flush left, and indent subsequent lines.

Bibliography

BIBLIOGRAPHY
Books

Marx, Wendy, and Simon Grenville. *Data Crunching in the Twenty-First Century.* Chicago: Sunshine Press, 1992.

Reynolds, Joseph. *Water Analysis.* New York: Technical Publications, 1987.

———. *Pollution Control.* New York: Technical Publications, 1986. [*a second book by the author above*]

Periodicals

Marah, Sarita. "Coliform Testing." *Journal of Microbiology* 19 (December, 1993): 244–245.

Von Cramm, S. H., et al. "Standards of Potability." *Hydrology Today* 142 (1989): 168–179. [*an article with several authors*]

Fig. 12.11

A reference list is less formal in style than a bibliography. It may give suggested readings and list source materials beyond those cited in the report itself. These may be grouped under headings referring to their topics; for example, "Books About *E. coli*" or "More Documents from the Tennessee Public Health Commission." The references need not include all of the information contained in a bibliographic reference; a title may suffice.

13

Agendas and Minutes

- Agendas
- Minutes
- Tips for Successful Meetings

Meetings are necessary. No organization of any size can proceed for long with each member acting independently. Meetings are held to discuss business, to explore ideas, and to convey information. An organized meeting can benefit the entire organization. A disorganized meeting can waste everyone's time. The difference lies in a few key strategies.

AGENDAS

An agenda informs people attending a meeting of the meeting's purpose and the business to be covered. Whether the meeting is 30 minutes or a week long, an agenda is designed to make sure the topics that need to be discussed are discussed and any extraneous business is left for another time. By following an agenda closely, the chairperson of a meeting can ensure that the meeting is purposeful and productive.

Any agenda must include the date of the meeting. The agenda for a short in-house meeting may simply list numbered topics to be discussed. The agenda for a longer meeting, such as a sales conference or stockholder's meeting, may be broken down into days and hours and include sites of individual sessions. Samples of each kind of agenda appear below.

Agenda for a Short Meeting

MEETING OF THE COUNTY DEMOCRATIC COMMITTEE
May 12, 1995 7:30 P.M.

1. Review and amend minutes.
2. Seat new members.
3. Hear report of highway subcommittee.
4. Vote on proposal to hold caucus.

Fig. 13.1

Agenda for a Long Meeting

SUMMER SALES CONFERENCE
Boca Raton, July 8–9

Thursday, July 8

8–10 A.M.	Working Breakfast	Cafeteria
10–11 A.M.	President's Greeting	Hall A
11 A.M.–Noon	Regional Managers' Meeting	Oyster Room
Noon–1 P.M.	Luncheon	Hall B
1 P.M.–3 P.M.	Exhibits	Main Floor
7 P.M.	Dinner Dance	Ballroom

Friday, July 9

8–9 A.M.	Working Breakfast	Cafeteria
9–11 A.M.	Regional Meetings	Rooms C–G
11 A.M.–Noon	Break	
Noon–1 P.M.	Luncheon	Hall B
1 P.M.–3 P.M.	"Making the Pitch" panel discussion Greg Lawford, chair	Hall A
3 P.M.–5 P.M.	Regional Workshops	Rooms C–G

Fig. 13.2

MINUTES

The minutes of a meeting are a written record of the business discussed and transacted at the meeting. Some companies tape record their meetings, and the tapes are transcribed and summarized. Most meetings, however, rely on a single person to record all events and decisions. If that person is you, follow these rules.

- Read the agenda before the meeting and keep it with you to serve as a guide.
- Make sure you know the names of all people who might speak. If someone speaks whose name you do not know, find out that person's name before the meeting adjourns.
- Sit close to the chairperson so that you are near the center of business.
- Use outline form or numbers or headings—whatever is most natural to you. Don't be afraid to mark up your notes with arrows and underlines if they help you organize your thoughts.
- Remember that the most important things to record are (1) those items on the agenda, (2) any major decisions or resolutions made by the attendees, and (3) the date and site of any future meeting. Formal resolutions should be recorded word for word.

Soon after the meeting adjourns, transcribe your notes into a first draft. Organize the draft by topic or time sequence, whichever seems more logical. If the draft must be approved by the chairperson or by your supervisor, take it to him or her as soon as possible. Make any changes and complete a final draft. Give it to the chairperson or your supervisor for signing, and distribute the minutes to whomever should receive them. Be sure to include anyone who was absent from the meeting on your distribution list. Keep a copy of the minutes on file, clipped to the agenda and any handouts for that meeting.

Minutes

MEETING OF THE COUNTY DEMOCRATIC COMMITTEE
May 12, 1995 7:30 P.M.

Attending were Dahlia Abrams (chairperson), Letitia Adair, Minnie Finn, Gloria Nu, Samuel Powers, Tim Powers, Andrew Quinn, Juanita Rodriguez, Stu Steinmetz, Ju-Lin Tao, and Wendy Watt.

The meeting was called to order at 7:35. Minnie Finn read the minutes from the April 15 meeting, and they were approved unanimously.

NEW MEMBERS
Dahlia Abrams proposed the seating of Wendy Watt and Tim Powers. Gloria Nu seconded. The members were approved and seated.

HIGHWAY SUBCOMMITTEE REPORT—ANDREW QUINN
Andrew Quinn reported that Route 13 will, as expected, be diverted for three months while the bridge in the village is repaired. A motion was made and seconded to review the plans with the town supervisor.

CAUCUS
Juanita Rodriguez proposed that we hold our town caucus to vote on nominees for the judgeship and county board members on Thursday, June 12. Sam Powers reminded the committee to call new voters from their registration lists to invite them to the caucus. Ms. Rodriguez's suggestion was seconded and approved. The caucus will take place Thursday, June 12, at 8 P.M. in Town Hall.

The meeting adjourned at 8:45. Our next meeting will follow the caucus on June 12.

Minnie Finn

Minnie Finn, Secretary

Fig. 13.3

TIPS FOR SUCCESSFUL MEETINGS

Following an agenda is certainly one key to a successful meeting, but there are other strategies that will guard against time-wasting and inefficiency.

- Make sure the site of your meeting is available. Book it well in advance and confirm it, in writing if necessary.
- Once the meeting site and date are firm, announce them to the attendees by memo or letter. Even if the meeting is held regularly on the third Wednesday of the month, a reminder notice may guarantee a full house. If possible, send a copy of the agenda at this time.
- If attendees are coming from far away, make sure their travel plans and accommodations are set. Confirm these.
- Check with speakers to see whether any audiovisual equipment or special materials are needed. If so, secure those materials and make sure that they work. If handouts are needed, you may have to supervise their preparation and make sure there are enough to go around, with an extra for your file.
- Stock a supply of paper and pens and extra agendas for attendees who forget to bring their own.

14

Itineraries

- Itineraries
- Tips for Successful Business Trips

Large companies have travel departments that coordinate business trips for company executives and other staff. In most places of business, however, the role of travel agent falls to the office assistant. It is not a difficult job if you are organized and plan ahead.

ITINERARIES

An itinerary is similar to an agenda. It tells travelers all they need to know about schedules, accommodations, and appointments related to their trip. As you plan the trip, take notes on all dates, times, and locations, so that you can incorporate these into the final itinerary.

An itinerary should include this information:

- departure times and locations for all transportation
- arrival times and locations for all transportation
- addresses of accommodations
- times and locations of all scheduled events or meetings
- names and phone numbers of relevant contacts

If the traveler will be passing through time zones, use the notations EST (Eastern Standard Time), CST (Central Standard Time), MST (Mountain Standard Time), PST (Pacific Standard Time), and so on beside any travel times on the itinerary. Use the time that corresponds to the location where the traveler will be.

With the itinerary, attach any airline, train, or bus tickets; hotel reservation confirmations and limousine vouchers; traveler's checks, if they are to be used; and agendas or programs for scheduled events. If the traveler needs to bring materials such as slides, files, speeches, and so on, those may be held with the itinerary as well, or shipped to the hotel ahead of time to be picked up on arrival.

Figure 14.1 is a sample itinerary for a two-day trip.

Itinerary

ITINERARY FOR KRISTIN WALKER
September 6–7

Thursday, September 6

8:10 A.M. EST	Leave Syracuse Airport via Continental Express Flight No. 2340. (all tickets attached)
10 A.M.	Arrive Pittsburgh Airport. Change planes.
10:35 A.M.	Leave Pittsburgh Airport via USAir Flight No. 141. (breakfast)
12:30 P.M. CST	Arrive Houston International Airport. Meet Sales Representative Don Juno (555-6575) at the gate; he will drive you to the Rio Rancho Resort on Alonzo Drive. (confirmation attached)
2:30 P.M.	Meet Don Juno out front for the trip to the Houston Board of Education.
3:15 P.M.	Presentation to Board of Education. Marla Perkins, chairperson Cindy Cochise, co-chair (slides and notes attached)
6:30 P.M.	Dinner with Regional Manager Philip Craig (555-0238). He will pick you up at your hotel.

Friday, September 7

9:15 A.M.	Meet Don Juno out front for drive to Barkeley Middle School.
10:30 A.M.	In-service for middle school teachers. (materials attached)
1:45 P.M.	Leave Houston International Airport via USAir Flight No. 202. (lunch)
6: 20 P.M. EST	Arrive Syracuse Airport.

Fig. 14.1

TIPS FOR SUCCESSFUL BUSINESS TRIPS

Once you have planned a few trips, you will settle into a comfortable routine. The first time, though, may be confusing. Here are some strategies to help you avoid conflict and chaos.

- Work with a reputable travel agent if possible. It costs you nothing, and it can save a great deal of time on the telephone.
- Obtain any cash advances or expense reports needed well in advance of the trip.
- If the traveler's materials are too heavy to take on board the plane, send them ahead by bus, air express, or UPS.
- Leave ample time between flights for plane changes, but try not to leave the traveler stranded at the airport for long periods of time.
- Confirm airline, hotel, and rental car reservations.
- For overseas travel, check on any need for visas, vaccination certificates, or international drivers' licenses. Make sure the traveler has a current passport. Try to change a small sum of money ahead of time, so that the traveler can pay for tips or small items on arrival.
- Photocopy all tickets and reservation confirmations. Keep them at the office with a list of traveler's check numbers in case the traveler's luggage is lost.

15

Mail Services

- Domestic Mail
- Special Services for Domestic Mail
- International Mail
- Special Services for International Mail
- Alternative Mail Services

Much of your written business communication is designed to be sent out of house. It is in your best interest to choose the most efficient means of delivery. This chapter introduces you to various delivery services and their regulations. For up-to-date rates, consult your post office or local delivery service.

DOMESTIC MAIL

To be mailable through the United States Postal Service, a piece of mail must be at least 7/1000 of an inch thick. Any piece of mail ¼ inch thick or less must be rectangular and at least 3½ inches high by 5 inches long. A piece greater than ¼ inch thick may measure less than 3½ by 5 inches.

Mail sent within the United States and its possessions should always be addressed using approved two-letter postal abbreviations for state and possession names and the five-digit ZIP code or ZIP + 4 code for the area. Here is a list of standard abbreviations.

Two-Letter State and Possession Abbreviations

State/Possession	Abbreviation	State/Possession	Abbreviation
Alabama	AL	Montana	MT
Alaska	AK	Nebraska	NE
Arkansas	AR	Nevada	NV
American Samoa	AS	New Hampshire	NH
California	CA	New Jersey	NJ
Colorado	CO	New Mexico	NM
Connecticut	CT	New York	NY
Delaware	DE	North Carolina	NC
District of Columbia	DC	North Dakota	ND
Federated States of Micronesia	FM	Northern Mariana Islands	MP
Florida	FL	Ohio	OH
Georgia	GA	Oklahoma	OK
Guam	GU	Oregon	OR
Hawaii	HI	Palau	PW
Idaho	ID	Pennsylvania	PA
Illinois	IL	Puerto Rico	PR
Indiana	IN	Rhode Island	RI
Iowa	IA	South Carolina	SC
Kansas	KS	South Dakota	SD
Kentucky	KY	Tennessee	TN
Louisiana	LA	Texas	TX
Maine	ME	Utah	UT
Marshall Islands	MH	Vermont	VT
Maryland	MD	Virginia	VA
Massachusetts	MA	Virgin Islands	VI
Michigan	MI	Washington	WA
Minnesota	MN	West Virginia	WV
Mississippi	MS	Wisconsin	WI
Missouri	MO	Wyoming	WY

Fig. 15.1

There are several classes of domestic mail. The one you choose depends on (1) what you are mailing and (2) how rapidly you would like the mail delivered.

• **First-Class Mail** may be a letter, a bill, a postcard, a greeting card, or a business reply card or letter. It costs the same no matter where in the United States it is sent. It must weigh 11 ounces or less and fulfill the mailability rules above. Since most mail now travels by air, it is unnecessary to specify "airmail" on a first-class piece traveling within the United States.

First-class mail is subject to a surcharge in addition to the regular stamp price if it exceeds ¼ inch in thickness, 11½ inches in length, or 6⅛ inches in width.

• **Priority Mail** is first-class mail that weighs more than 11 ounces but less than 70 pounds. The cost of mailing priority mail that weighs over 2 pounds is determined by zone and by weight; that is, it costs more to send priority mail far away than it does to send it to a local address, and it costs more to send a heavy package than a light one. Special Priority Mail envelopes for 2-pound mailings are available from the post office.

• **Second-Class Mail** is a special rate available only to newspapers and periodicals that have second-class authorization. To qualify, pieces must be published at least four times annually, and they may not be advertising circulars. For other regulations and restrictions, talk to your local post office.

• **Third-Class Mail** may include circulars, catalogs, photographs, other printed matter, or merchandise weighing less than 16 ounces.

Third-Class Bulk Rates are available for organizations that send out a minimum of 200 pieces of the same type at one time. For example, advertising circulars or annual reports may be sent bulk rate. To obtain this special rate, you must apply to the local post office and fill out a set of forms. You will receive a bulk mail number, which you can then make into a permit imprint to be printed on the upper right-hand corner of your bulk mail (see Figure 15.2). The mail must be sorted according to

ZIP codes and labeled with preprinted labels the post office wil
provide. For each shipment, you must bring the sorted mail t
the bulk mail window of the post office and fill out a statemen
of mailing.

Nonprofit Third-Class Bulk Rates are available only t
organizations and agencies that are issued a special rate autho
rization by the Postal Service. A qualified nonprofit organiza
tion can save over 50% off first-class stamp prices if it sends it
newsletters and other bulk materials with this special rate. Th
sorting and labeling of mail follow the third-class bulk mai
regulations described above.

Bulk Mail Permit Imprints

BULK RATE U.S. POSTAGE PAID DOVER DE PERMIT NO. 000	NONPROFIT ORG. U.S. POSTAGE PAID MILWAUKEE WI PERMIT NO. 000

Fig. 15.2

- **Fourth-Class Mail** is more commonly known as parce
post. It is used for materials that weigh more than 16 ounces bu
less than 70 pounds. The cost of mailing is determined both b
weight and by zone.

Special Fourth-Class Rates are available for mailing book
films, printed music, educational and test materials, scripts an
manuscripts, and medical information. Consult your post offic
to see whether your materials qualify for these rates.

Bound Printed Matter Rates can be used to mail bound (nc
looseleaf) promotional or educational materials.

Library Rates are available for books, unpublished manu
scripts, periodicals, and other printed or recorded matter that i

shipped between educational institutions, museums, libraries, or qualified nonprofit organizations.

• **Express Mail** is an overnight delivery service provided by the Postal Service for mailable items up to 70 pounds in weight and 108 inches in combined length and girth. You must fill out an Express Mail form for each item to be mailed. Items may be picked up at your office or mailed from the post office. Depending on your instructions, the item will be delivered to the addressee by noon or 3 P.M. the following business day. Any merchandise is automatically insured to a maximum of $500.

• **Official Mail** is mail sent between certain employees of the United States government. It requires no postage.

Franked Mail carries a facsimile of the employee's signature in place of the stamp. This kind of mail can only be used by representatives of the highest levels of government.

Penalty Mail is marked "Penalty for Private Use to Avoid Payment of Postage" and "Official Business" and may be used by government agencies for official correspondence only.

SPECIAL SERVICES FOR DOMESTIC MAIL

If you wish to take advantage of any of the special services provided by the United States Postal Service, you must go to a post office. All special services charge a fee, and all require filling out of forms.

• **Certificate of Mailing** can be requested if you need proof that you mailed an item. This certificate does *not* prove that the item was received by the addressee.

• **Certified Mail** is used to send first-class or priority mail when you want to be positive the mail is received by the addressee. There is a fee for certified mail, but this does not insure your mailed materials. Valuables should not be mailed by this method. You may ask for a return receipt to ensure delivery. This is essentially a post card that you address to yourself, which is delivered to you when the mail you sent is received by the addressee.

• **Collect on Delivery** is used to send first-class, third-class, fourth-class, or express mail, when the addressee is asked to pay for the items at the time of delivery. When you mail something COD, you pay for the postage and insurance. At this writing, the maximum allowable value for COD items is $600. The items may be paid for by check made out to the sender, or by cash, in which case the Postal Service issues the sender a money order.

• **Insurance** is available for third-class or fourth-class items worth up to $600, for a fee equal to about 1 or 2 percent of the insurance coverage. You must fill out both sides of the form shown below.

• **Money Orders** are negotiable instruments similar to checks that may be purchased, redeemed, or transferred at the post office.

• **Registered Mail** is used to mail any first-class, priority, or COD items of value. By registering your mail, you enable it to be tracked at all points along its route, adding to the delivery time, but also safeguarding the material against loss. To protect your mail further, the Postal Service requires that you seal your mail along all edges with package sealing tape or cloth tape. For extremely valuable items, you may request additional insurance, and you may ask for a return receipt.

• **Restricted Delivery** is something you can request if you want a COD, certified, insured, or registered item delivered to a specific person. This service is not available for items insured for less than $50, nor is it available for Express Mail. The addressee will be asked for proof of identification.

• **Special Delivery** is available for all classes of mail, but it only applies to mail sent within a certain distance of a given post office. If you have mail that you want delivered quickly (before regular mail) on a business day to a place not far away, special delivery may be helpful. The fee does not cover insurance, so be sure to insure valuables before sending them special delivery.

• **Special Handling** is available for third-class and fourth-class mail, whether or not it is sent COD or insured. Use it for packages that are fragile or easily damaged, and it will ensure special treatment.

INTERNATIONAL MAIL

Rates for mailing materials to Canada and Mexico are figured differently from rates for mailing to other parts of the world. When you mail a package to Canada, use the approved National Postal Code abbreviation for the province or territory. Here is a list of those abbreviations.

Two-Letter Province and Territory Abbreviations

Alberta	AB	Northwest Territories	NT
British Columbia	BC	Ontario	ON
Labrador	LB	Prince Edward Island	PE
Manitoba	MB	Quebec	PQ
New Brunswick	NB	Saskatchewan	SK
Newfoundland	NF	Yukon Territory	YT
Nova Scotia	NS		

Fig. 15.3

There are three main categories of international mail and a few express and bulk mailing options.

• **LC Mail** consists of letters, letter packages, aerogrammes, and post cards. The weight limit is 4 pounds, but registered items sent to Canada may weigh as much as 66 pounds. All mail of this class sent to Canada or Mexico goes by air. For mail sent overseas, there are two rates—airmail and surface mail. The difference in price is substantial, but so is the difference in time. If you need something shipped quickly, do not use surface mail.

• **AO Mail** consists of printed matter, books, sheet music, periodicals, small packets, and material for the blind. The weight limit varies from country to country depending on what is being mailed; consult the post office to see what the requirements are for your particular materials. Surface rates and airmail rates are available for this class of mail to Canada, Mexico, and overseas.

M-Bag or Sack Mail is an option if you are sending a large quantity of books or printed matter (from 15 to 66 pounds) to a single addressee. The post office will help you arrange for this special packaging; the requirements are stringent and must be overseen by a postal inspector.

• **CP Mail** is parcel post, and resembles fourth-class domestic mail. Weight limits and rates depend on the country to which you are mailing materials. Both surface and airmail rates are available.

• **Express Mail International Service** includes insurance and a mailing receipt, and offers high-speed service to many countries.

• **Intelpost** offers same or next-day delivery of facsimile documents from post offices in many U.S. cities to certain foreign destinations.

• **International Priority Airmail Service** is designed for bulk mailing of LC or AO mail. The post office can help you prepare bulk mailings of this kind.

• **International Surface Air Lift** is a bulk mailing system for sending advertising circulars, periodicals, catalogs, and other printed matter. You pay per pound or per piece, depending on the destination and the contents.

SPECIAL SERVICES FOR INTERNATIONAL MAIL

Certified and COD services are not available for international mail, but most other special services are provided with certain restrictions.

• **Insurance** is available for parcel post (CP) items. Limits on indemnity vary depending on the country where the package is being sent.

• **Money Orders** may be transmitted to most locations. Check with your post office.

• **Registered Mail** is available to all countries, but the post office liability is limited to $32.35 except on packages sent to Canada. You may ask for a return receipt to ensure delivery.

• **Restricted Delivery** is available for registered items that you wish to have delivered to a specific person.

• **Special Delivery** is available for LC and AO mail. Its cost depends on the weight of the material.

• **Special Handling** is available for surface printed matter, small packets, or parcel post. There are two rates: one for material weighing 10 pounds or less and one for material weighing over 10 pounds.

ALTERNATIVE MAIL SERVICES

Check your telephone directory for alternative delivery services available in your area. Possibilities are listed below.

• **Messenger Services** can save you money and ensure immediate delivery. They are useful if you have a constant flow of local deliveries and pick-ups. Most urban messenger services rely on bicycles or public transportation. You can arrange to have pickups and deliveries made at a set time each day, or you can ask the messenger service to be on call for your varying needs.

• **Ground Services** offer rapid, tracked delivery of items of all sizes by surface transportation. United Parcel Service and Purolator are two companies that provide this service. You may also send heavy materials by bus from station to station. Check with your local bus companies for a list of fees, services, weight guidelines, destinations, and timetables.

• **Air Services** are, obviously, faster than ground services. Many offer next-day delivery of packages throughout the United States and to foreign destinations as well. The cost of delivery depends on the size of the package and the speed at which you want it delivered. United Parcel Service has expanded into the air business and competes with such companies as Federal Express and AirExpress. Some airlines will ship packages for you as well from airport to airport. Check with your local airlines for availability and cost of this service.

III

Communicating Electronically

16

Telephones

- Telephone Manners: Incoming Calls
- Telephone Manners: Outgoing Calls
- Basic Telephone Services
- Special Telephone Services
- Equipment

A tremendous amount of business takes place over the telephone. Often the only contact a client has with your company is with your disembodied voice at the end of the telephone line. Whether you work in a two-person office or a multinational corporation, your telephone skills must be flawless.

TELEPHONE MANNERS: INCOMING CALLS

Your job may often involve serving as your company's representative—the first person to whom a caller speaks. Whether the caller receives a good impression of your company depends on your handling of the call. The list below contains tips on handling incoming calls.

1. Answer Promptly.

You hate wasting time waiting for the phone to be answered, and so do your company's clients. Answer on the first or second ring, if possible. State your company name or the name of your supervisor, if that is whose phone you are answering. Then state your name:

"Good morning. Winslow-Bates Corporation. This is Ms. Ferger."
"Hello. Mr. Crispell's office. Shelley Ferger speaking."

2. Use "Hold" Politely.

If you must put someone on hold to deal with another call or search for information, ask first.

"May I put you on hold?"
"Will you hold, or would you like to call back?"

Return within the minute to assure the caller that you have not abandoned him or her.

3. Identify the Caller.

Some callers do not introduce themselves. As soon as you can do so politely, interject:

"Who may I say is calling?"
"May I tell Mr. Crispell who is calling?"

4. Screen Calls If Necessary.

Your supervisor may like to have you answer all incoming calls and direct important calls only to her or him. You must work out together which types of calls are to be passed on and which you should deal with, postpone, or transfer elsewhere. In screening calls, you must be sure to identify the caller and the purpose of the call early on. Then use the appropriate response:

> **"Mr. Crispell is in a meeting. Perhaps I can help you."**
> **"Mr. Crispell is on another line. May I have him call you back? What is a convenient time for you? May I take your number?"**
> **"Ms. Del Rio is in charge of promotion. Her direct number is 555-1727. If you like, I will transfer you to her department."**

5. Transfer Calls Competently.

All of us have been cut off at times in the middle of a transferred call. Make sure you know how to use your office equipment. After you reach the department you want, identify the caller and his or her business to the person who answers. Then stay on the line long enough to make sure the call went through.

6. Take Accurate Messages.

Keep a record of incoming calls whether you are answering the phone for someone else or for yourself. Many companies require accurate record-keeping of all long-distance calls, but even local calls may be important to record. If you are taking a message for someone else, include these points.

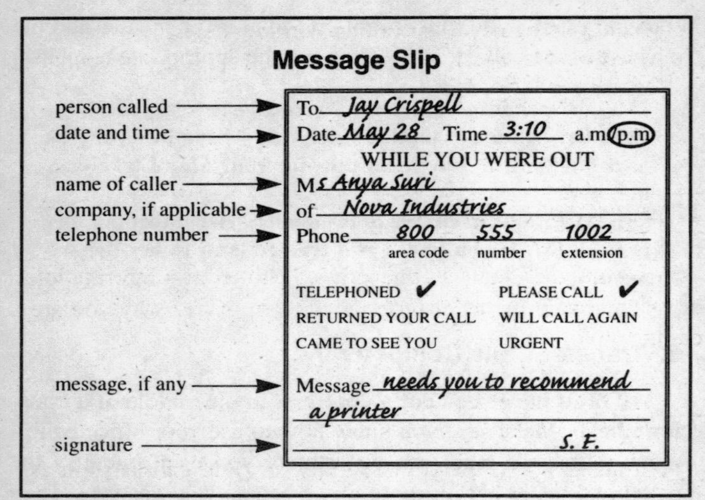

Fig. 16.1

7. Promise Prompt Action, and Follow Up.

If you said that your supervisor would call back, make sure he or she has the information to do so. If you promised to locate information and get back to the caller, do so as soon as possible. If you agreed to check with your supervisor in order to make an appointment for her or him, do so as soon as your supervisor is available. (Never make an appointment for someone else without checking in person first. Not all executives list everything on their calendars.)

8. Disconnect Politely.

Do not simply hang up on a caller. The caller should always be given the privilege of saying "goodbye" first and hanging up first. You may respond to his or her "goodbye" in one of several ways:

"Goodbye. Thank you for calling Winslow-Bates."
"Goodbye, Ms. Suri."
"Thank you for calling."

TELEPHONE MANNERS: OUTGOING CALLS

Your outgoing calls will generally be to request information or make appointments or reservations. No matter why you are calling, courtesy is key.

1. Identify Yourself.

Introduce yourself and the purpose of your call as soon as the call is picked up.

"Hello. This is Shelley Ferger from Winslow-Bates. May I please speak to Mrs. Levi?"
"Hello. This is Shelley Ferger. I am calling to check on the hotel reservations for Mr. Crispell for next Thursday, June 5."

2. Speak Clearly and Vary Your Pitch.

A drone does not carry well over the telephone line. If you mumble into the receiver, you will not be heard on the other end. Enunciate clearly, sound cheerful and interested, and speak directly into the phone.

3. Know What You are Going to Say.

Before you call, make a plan. Know the person's name to whom you must speak and know what questions you wish to ask. If necessary, make notes in advance and have them with you as you make your call. You do not want to have to call back with questions you forgot to ask earlier.

4. Take Notes.

Do not make the person on the other end repeat names, dates, or numbers—take notes as he or she speaks. If you have made advance notes, check off your questions as you ask them and write each answer next to the question.

BASIC TELEPHONE SERVICES

Depending on your office's telephone network, you may simply dial a four-digit extension to reach someone in the building. To get an outside line, you may need to dial a one-digit code. Local telephone numbers contain seven digits. To place a call outside your local calling area, you have several choices of service.

- **Direct Distance Dialing** allows you to bypass an operator and dial the long-distance number directly. You will be charged for the call no matter who answers the phone, even if the call is picked up by an answering service or machine. To call within your area code, dial 1 + the seven-digit telephone number. To call outside your area code, dial 1 + the three-digit area code + the seven-digit telephone number. Various long-distance services require you to dial a code in addition to the number. Make sure you know which long-distance company your company uses.

Area Codes for Some Major Locations

ALABAMA	205
ALASKA	907
ARIZONA	602
ARKANSAS	501
Bahamas	809
Bermuda	809
CALIFORNIA	
Alhambra	818
Anaheim	714
Bakersfield	805
Berkeley	510
Corona	909
Fresno	209
Los Angeles	213, 310
Oakland	510
Orange	714
Pasadena	818
Sacramento	916
San Diego	619
San Francisco	415
San Jose	408
Santa Barbara	805
Santa Rosa	707
Stockton	209
Whittier	310, 818
COLORADO	
Colorado Springs	719
Denver	303
Pueblo	719
CONNECTICUT	203
DELAWARE	302
DISTRICT OF COLUMBIA	
Washington, DC	202
FLORIDA	
Jacksonville	904
Miami	305
Orlando	407
St. Petersburg	813
Tallahassee	904
Tampa	813
West Palm Beach	407
GEORGIA	
Atlanta	404
Augusta	706
Macon	912
Savannah	912
HAWAII	808
IDAHO	208
ILLINOIS	
Alton	708
Chicago	312
Evanston	708
Joliet	815
Marion	618
Peoria	309
Springfield	217
Waukegan	708
INDIANA	
Evansville	812
Gary	219
Indianapolis	317
South Bend	219
Terre Haute	812
IOWA	
Cedar Rapids	319
Des Moines	515
Sioux City	712
KANSAS	
Kansas City	913
Topeka	913
Wichita	316
KENTUCKY	
Covington	606

Lexington	606
Louisville	502
LOUISIANA	
New Orleans	504
Shreveport	318
MAINE	207
MARYLAND	
Baltimore	410
Cumberland	301
Frederick	301
MASSACHUSETTS	
Boston	617
Springfield	413
Worcester	508
MICHIGAN	
Battle Creek	616
Detroit	313
Escanaba	906
Grand Rapids	616
Lansing	517
Marquette	906
Saginaw	517
MINNESOTA	
Duluth	218
Minneapolis	612
Rochester	507
St. Paul	612
MISSISSIPPI	601
MISSOURI	
Kansas City	816
St. Louis	314
Springfield	417
MONTANA	406
NEBRASKA	
Grand Island	308
Omaha	402
NEVADA	702
NEW HAMPSHIRE	603
NEW JERSEY	
Elizabeth	908
Newark	201
New Brunswick	908
Trenton	609
NEW MEXICO	505
NEW YORK	
Albany	518
Amityville	516
Auburn	315
Binghamton	607
Brooklyn	718
Brewster	914
Bronx	718
Bronxville	914
Buffalo	716
Long Island	516
Manhattan	212
Queens	718
Staten Island	718
Syracuse	315
White Plains	914
NORTH CAROLINA	
Asheville	704
Charlotte	704
Fayetteville	919
Greensboro	910
Raleigh	919
NORTH DAKOTA	701
OHIO	
Cincinnati	513
Cleveland	216
Columbus	614
Toledo	419
OKLAHOMA	
Oklahoma City	405
Tulsa	918
OREGON	503
PENNSYLVANIA	
Altoona	814

Bethlehem	610	Ft. Worth	817
Erie	814	Galveston	409
Harrisburg	717	Houston	713
Philadelphia	215	San Antonio	210
Pittsburgh	412	Sheppard Air Force Base	817
Sharon	412	UTAH	801
PUERTO RICO	809	VERMONT	802
RHODE ISLAND	401	VIRGIN ISLANDS	809
SOUTH CAROLINA	803	VIRGINIA	
SOUTH DAKOTA	605	Arlington	703
TENNESSEE		Richmond	804
Chattanooga	615	WASHINGTON	
Memphis	901	Seattle	206
Nashville	615	Spokane	509
TEXAS		WEST VIRGINIA	304
Amarillo	806	WISCONSIN	
Austin	512	Eau Claire	715
Corpus Christi	512	Madison	608
Dallas	214	Milwaukee	414
Denison	903	Wausau	715
El Paso	915	WYOMING	307

Fig. 16.2

Keep in mind the time differences when you make long distance calls. When it is noon in New York City, it is 11 A.M. in Chicago, 10 A.M. in Denver, 9 A.M. in Los Angeles, 8 A.M. in Anchorage, and only 7 A.M. in Honolulu.

• **Collect Calls** may be made to a person or station that agrees to accept the call and pay the charges. You are most likely to make such a call from outside your company back to your own office. Dial 0 + the number to make a collect call. Inform the operator that you wish to place a collect call.

• **Conference Calls** allow you to speak to people in different places at the same time. You can make an in-house conference call by going through the PBX (private branch exchange) switchboard. To place an external conference call, dial 0 and arrange the call with the operator. You will need to tell the operator the telephone numbers involved and a time at which the call should be placed.

• **Mobile Calls** may be made to automobiles, trucks, aircraft, boats, and ships. Dial 0 and ask the operator to connect you to the Mobile Operator, the Marine Operator, or the High Seas Operator.

• **Operator-Assisted Station-to-Station Dialing** is useful if you do not care who answers the phone. If you need operator assistance in placing the call, you will be charged somewhat more than if you use direct distance dialing. Coin phone calls, collect calls, calling card calls, calls billed to a third number, and calls where you request time and charges are examples of calls where operator assistance might be required.

• **Overseas Calls** may be made directly by dialing 011 + the country code + the city code + the number. If you need operator assistance, dial 01 + the country code + the city code + the number.

Country and City Codes

Country	Code	Time Difference
ALGERIA†	**213**	**+6**
AMERICAN SAMOA†	**684**	**–6**
ARGENTINA	**54**	**+2**
Buenos Aires	1	
ARUBA	**297**	**+1**
AUSTRALIA	**61**	**+15**
Melbourne	3	
Sydney	2	
AUSTRIA	**43**	**+6**
Vienna	1	

† City codes not required

†† Seven-digit numbers: dial country code only. Six-digit numbers: dial country and city codes.

BAHRAIN	**973**	**+8**
BANGLADESH	**880**	**+11**
BELGIUM	**32**	**+6**
Antwerp	3	
Brussels	2	
BELIZE	**501**	**–1**
BOLIVIA	**591**	**+1**
La Paz	2	
BRAZIL	**55**	**+2**
Brasilia	61	
Rio de Janeiro	21	
São Paulo	11	
CAMEROON†	**237**	**+6**
CHILE	**56**	**+1**
Santiago	2	
CHINA	**86**	**+13**
Beijing (Peking)	1	
Guangzhou (Canton)	20	
Shanghai	21	
COLOMBIA	**57**	**0**
Bogota	1	
COSTA RICA†	**506**	**–1**
CYPRUS	**357**	**+7**
CZECH REPUBLIC	**42**	**+6**
Prague	2	
DENMARK	**45**	**+6**
Copenhagen	1 or 2	
ECUADOR	**593**	**0**
Guayaquil	4	
Quito	2	
EGYPT	**20**	**+7**
Alexandria	3	
Cairo	2	
EL SALVADOR†	**503**	**–1**
ETHIOPIA	**251**	**+8**
Addis Ababa	1	
FIJI†	**679**	**+17**
FINLAND	**358**	**+7**
Helsinki	0	

FRANCE	**33**	**+6**
Marseille	91	
Lyon	7	
Paris	13, 14, or 16	
FRENCH ANTILLES†	**596**	**+1**
FRENCH POLYNESIA†	**689**	**–5**
GABON†	**241**	**+6**
GERMANY	**49**	**+6**
Berlin	30	
Frankfurt	69	
Munich	89	
GHANA	**233**	**+5**
GREECE	**30**	**+7**
Athens	1	
GUADELOUPE†	**590**	**+1**
GUAM†	**671**	**+15**
GUANTANAMO BAY†	**53**	**0**
All points	99	
GUATEMALA	**502**	**–1**
Guatemala City	2	
GUYANA	**592**	**+2**
HAITI	**509**	**0**
Port au Prince	1	
HONDURAS†	**504**	**–1**
HONG KONG††	**852**	**+13**
HUNGARY	**36**	**+6**
Budapest	1	
ICELAND	**354**	**+5**
Reykjavik	1	
INDIA	**91**	**+10½**
Bombay	22	
Calcutta	33	
New Delhi	11	
INDONESIA	**62**	**+12**
Jakarta	21	
IRAN	**98**	**+8½**
Teheran	21	
IRAQ	**964**	**+8**
Baghdad	1	

IRELAND	**353**	**+5**
Dublin	1	
ISRAEL	**972**	**+7**
Jerusalem	2	
Tel Aviv	3	
ITALY	**39**	**+6**
Florence	55	
Milan	2	
Naples	81	
Rome	6	
IVORY COAST†	**225**	**+5**
JAPAN	**81**	**+14**
Osaka	6	
Tokyo	3	
Yokohama	45	
JORDAN	**962**	**+7**
Amman	6	
KENYA	**254**	**+8**
Nairobi	2	
KOREA, REP. OF	**82**	**+14**
Pusan	51	
Seoul	2	
KUWAIT†	**965**	**+8**
LIBERIA†	**231**	**+5**
LIBYA	**218**	**+7**
Tripoli	21	
LIECHTENSTEIN	**41**	**+6**
All points	75	
LUXEMBOURG†	**352**	**+6**
MALAWI	**265**	**+7**
MALAYSIA	**60**	**+13**
Kuala Lumpur	3	
MALI†	**223**	**+5**
MALTA†	**356**	**+6**
MEXICO	**52**	**–1**
Guadalajara	36	
Mexico City	5	
MONACO	**33**	**+6**
All points	93	

MOROCCO	**212**	**+5**
Casablanca†		
NAMIBIA	**264**	**+7**
NEPAL†	**977**	**+10½**
NETHERLANDS	**31**	**+6**
Amsterdam	20	
Rotterdam	10	
The Hague	70	
ANTILLES	**599**	**+1**
NEW CALEDONIA†	**687**	**+16**
NEW ZEALAND	**64**	**+17**
Auckland	9	
Wellington	4	
NICARAGUA	**505**	**–1**
Managua	2	
NIGERIA	**234**	**+6**
Lagos	1	
NORWAY	**47**	**+6**
Bergen	5	
Oslo	2	
OMAN†	**968**	**+9**
PAKISTAN	**92**	**+10**
Islamabad	51	
Karachi	21	
PANAMA†	**507**	**0**
PAPUA NEW GUINEA†	**675**	**+15**
PARAGUAY	**595**	**+2**
Asuncion	21	
PERU	**51**	**0**
Lima	14	
PHILIPPINES	**63**	**+13**
Manila	2	
POLAND	**48**	**+6**
Warsaw	22	
PORTUGAL	**351**	**+5**
Lisbon	1	
QATAR†	**974**	**+8**
ROMANIA	**40**	**+7**
Bucharest	0	

RUSSIA	**7**	**+8** (western)
Moscow	095	
SAIPAN†	**670**	**+15**
SAN MARINO	**39**	**+6**
All points	541	
SAUDIA ARABIA	**966**	**+8**
Riyadh	1	
SENEGAL†	**221**	**+5**
SINGAPORE†	**65**	**+13**
SLOVAKIA	**42**	**+6**
SOUTH AFRICA	**27**	**+7**
Cape Town	21	
Johannesburg	11	
Pretoria	12	
SPAIN	**34**	**+6**
Barcelona	3	
Madrid	1	
Seville	54	
SRI LANKA	**94**	**+10½**
Colombo	1	
SURINAME†	**597**	**+2**
SWEDEN	**46**	**+6**
Goteborg	31	
Stockholm	8	
SWITZERLAND	**41**	**+6**
Berne	31	
Geneva	22	
Zurich	1	
TAIWAN	**886**	**+13**
Taipei	2	
TANZANIA	**255**	**+8**
THAILAND	**66**	**+12**
Bangkok	2	
TUNISIA	**216**	**+6**
TURKEY	**90**	**+7**
Ankara	4	
Istanbul	1	
UNITED ARAB EMIRATES	**971**	**+9**
Abu Dhabi	2	

Dubai	4	
UNITED KINGDOM	**44**	**+5**
Belfast	232	
Birmingham	21	
Glasgow	41	
London	71 or 81	
URUGUAY	**598**	**+2**
Montevideo	2	
VATICAN CITY	**39**	**+6**
All points	6	
VENEZUELA	**58**	**+1**
Caracas	2	
Maracaibo	61	
YEMEN ARAB REPUBLIC	**967**	**+8**
Sanaa	2	
YUGOSLAVIA	**38**	**+6**
Belgrade	11	
ZAIRE	**243**	**+6**
ZIMBABWE	**263**	**+7**

Fig. 16.3

• **Person-to-Person Dialing** allows you to talk to a specific person. You are assisted by the operator and do not pay unless you reach the party you specify. Dial 0 + the seven-digit number for calls within your area code, or 0 + the three-digit area code + the seven-digit number for calls outside your area code. Inform the operator that you wish to place a person-to-person call.

• **Wide Area Telecommunications Service (WATS)** allows businesses to receive station-to-station calls from clients without charge to the client. It also allows businesses to make unlimited station-to-station calls within a given geographic area at one monthly rate. Businesses must subscribe to this service. WATS numbers begin with the prefix 800.

• **Directory Assistance** is available for a fee when you do not know the number of the person or firm you are calling. For numbers within your area code, dial 555-1212. For numbers outside your area code, dial 1 + the three-digit area code + 555-1212. For 800 numbers, dial 1 + 800 + 555-1212. For international calls, dial 00.

SPECIAL TELEPHONE SERVICES

A number of time-saving special services are available through your telephone company.

• **Call Forwarding** enables you to transfer incoming calls automatically to another telephone anywhere in the continental United States.

• **Call Waiting** sends a tone through the line when you are talking to one party and a second party calls. You can then place the first party on hold to answer the second call.

• **Speed Calling** lets you program in frequently-dialed numbers so that you can call them simply by dialing one or two digits.

• **Three-Way Calling** allows you to add a third party to your conversation. With this service, you can make three-way conference calls without the assistance of an operator.

EQUIPMENT

Telecommunications equipment is changing so rapidly that any system purchased one year may be obsolete the next. Some of the apparatus and systems available are listed below. Many new systems incorporate most or all of the following.

• **Call Directors** are simple switchboards that allow one person to pick up calls for many extensions. One office assistant can use a call director to answer and transfer calls for an entire department.

• **Centrex** is a direct internal dialing system; in other words calls do not go through a switchboard. All of the telephone numbers in the Centrex system have the same three-digit prefix so to dial in-house, you need only dial a two- or four-digit extension.

• **Computerized Branch Exchange (CBX)** is an expansion of the Centrex system, offering special services such as call forwarding, call waiting, three-way calling, and automatic transfers.

• **Multiline Phones** are even simpler than switchboards, but they serve the same purpose for up to 30 separate phone extensions. The phone has a button for each extension, and the buttons light up when the extension is in use. Calls can be put on hold and transferred from a single phone.

• **Private Branch Exchange (PBX)** systems run all calls through a central switchboard. An operator within the building connects incoming calls with office extensions. To call out, employees dial a one-digit code (for example, 9) before direct-dialing an outside telephone number or dialing 0 to reach an outside operator.

• **Private Automatic Branch Exchange (PABX)** systems are automated PBX systems. Often, no operator is needed to connect calls.

• **Speakerphones** allow you to speak to a caller from anywhere in the room without lifting the receiver. A microphone amplifies your voice, and speakers broadcast your caller's voice. Speakerphones are useful when more than one person wish to listen to or speak to a caller.

• **Voice Mail** stores messages digitally. The caller hears a recording asking for a message. The system dials ahead and delivers the message in the caller's voice or stores it for later delivery. You may dial your voice-mail number at any time to hear your messages. Your supervisor may want you to transfer her or his voice mail messages onto written message memos so that she or he may have them at her or his disposal.

17

Telegrams, Telexes, and Cablegrams

- Telegrams
- Telexes
- Cablegrams

On occasion you will need to transmit written information quickly. If the receiving party has a facsimile machine, that may be the easiest option. If that is not an option, however, you may send a telegram, telex, or cablegram.

TELEGRAMS

A **telegram** is a written message sent from one telegraphy machine to another. The most common kind of telegraphy system is called *Telex*. If your company or the party receiving the message does not have a Telex machine, you must send a telegram *via* a telegraphy company, most likely Western Union.

Western Union can take your message by telephone or by Telex. They can deliver it orally or in writing. They can also wire travelers' checks or money orders.

For telegrams sent within the United States, you will be

charged per word, no matter how long the word might be. You will not be charged for punctuation marks. The symbols @ and ¢ cannot be transmitted.

Telegrams are expensive compared to telephone calls or faxes. You can cut costs by sending night telegrams, to be delivered the following morning, and by eliminating unnecessary words. Do not worry about writing complete sentences; try to convey your meaning in as few words as possible.

Telegram

Date: August 1, 1995
To: Centermart Corporation
Care of: Roy Alvarez
Address and
Telephone Number: 100 Perimeter Center
Atlanta, GA 30346
(404) 555-2525

NEED GROSSMAN PROJECT BID ASAP.
WILL CALL TOMORROW

Sender: John Q. Public
Address and
daytime phone number: Delta Realty
636 Third Avenue
New York, N.Y. 10022
(212) 598-1111

Fig. 17.1

TELEXES

Nowadays, many large companies have their own telegraphy equipment. You can send a **telex** (like a telegram) directly to such a company by using your Telex system. Most systems include a teleprinter and a dialing apparatus similar to that found on a telephone. You type your message and dial the number of the recipient's Telex. You are charged for the service in the same way you would be charged for a telephone call—by the time taken to transmit rather than by the number of words.

CABLEGRAMS

Cablegrams are telegrams sent overseas by way of undersea cable. You can use your Telex system to send a cablegram, or you may use Western Union or another telegraphy service. For telegrams sent overseas by Western Union, long words cost more than short words, and most punctuation marks and symbols may not be used. Rates depend on the distance the cablegram will travel as well as the number of words in the message. Full-rate cablegrams may be sent in code. Cablegrams sent at night for next-day delivery must be written in words, but any foreign language may be used.

18

Faxes

- Basic Fax Features
- Special Fax Features
- Fax Modems
- Tips for Successful Fax Transmission

The cheapest and most convenient way to send written information quickly is by facsimile transmission, or fax. In addition to contracts and typewritten manuscripts, facsimile machines can reproduce photographs and drawings, making them useful for any kind of black-and-white document transmission.

BASIC FAX FEATURES

To use a fax machine, you feed a document into the document feeder and dial the telephone number of the fax machine you want to receive the document. A scanner scans the document and translates it into units of light and dark. The electronic representation of the document is then transmitted over telephone lines to another fax machine, which decodes the scanned image and represents it on paper.

Fax machines may use thermal paper, which comes in rolls,

or they may use plain paper. Some fax machines that use rolls have automatic paper cutters built in. Expensive machines recreate halftones (shades of gray) better than cheaper models do. A document having a lot of halftones will take longer to transmit, simply because the scanner must do more work to translate the image.

SPECIAL FAX FEATURES

Many fax machines have special features that speed transmission and eliminate lines at the fax machine.

- **Automatic Send** allows you to load documents and send them at off-peak hours when phone rates are lower.
- **Batch Transmission** configures your fax to store documents in files and send an entire batch at a time specified by you.
- **Broadcasting** is useful if you must send a document to more than one long-distance recipient. Your fax machine holds the document in memory and calls the recipient fax machines automatically at a time you designate.
- **Collated Reception** means that as your transmitter sends pages in numerical order, your fax prints them face down, thereby collating them and eliminating the need to sort the completed fax.
- **Dual Access** allows you to store documents in memory with instructions about where to send them at the same time that the fax is receiving or transmitting another document. This is a time-saving device for busy offices—the machine can hold several documents in memory and will transmit them in the order received.
- **Duplex Faxing** saves paper by enabling you to transmit two-sided documents.
- **Error Correction Mode** automatically corrects errors caused by noise on the telephone line.

• **Polling** lets your fax machine call another fax machine at off-peak hours, give it an ID code, and ask it if it has a transmission. If the ID code is correct and there is a transmission to send, the second fax will transmit at that time.

• **Quick Scan** scans documents into memory up to four times faster than standard fax machines can. It is used in conjunction with dual access to enable a transmitter to prepare documents for transmission as quickly as possible.

FAX MODEMS

A **fax modem** is a circuit card that fits into a computer. Along with its accompanying software and a telephone jack, it turns your computer into a fax machine while eliminating the intermediate step: the paper. You can transmit images directly from your computer screen to another fax machine or to a fax-equipped computer. For more on modems, see Chapter 26.

TIPS FOR SUCCESSFUL FAX TRANSMISSION

No two brands of fax machine are exactly alike. Your operation manual will alert you to the corrective measures you should take if your unit fails to transmit or receive. These tips will help ensure successful transmission.

- Remove all staples or paper clips from documents.
- Place wrinkled, torn, or small documents in a clear plastic carrier.
- Some fax machines load documents face down; others load them face up. Check your manual before proceeding.
- If you are transmitting manually, wait for the distinctive fax tone on the other end before you hit your transmit button.

- Check your settings to make sure you are transmitting efficiently. Most faxes have different MODE settings for standard resolution (regular typed documents), fine resolution (documents with some detail), or half-tones (photographs and detailed drawings).

19

E-Mail

- Basic E-Mail Features
- Special E-Mail Features
- Tips for Successful E-mail Transmission

E-mail, or electronic mail, may refer to telegrams, telexes, faxes, and so on. Most often, however, the term is used to mean message systems that transmit from one computer to another via telephone lines and modems or interconnected computer networks.

BASIC E-MAIL FEATURES

Computer-based E-mail systems are usually found in large corporations with a number of branch offices. Within a single building, terminals may be linked up to a main computer, which stores messages transmitted from terminals. Workers may check their "Electronic mailbox" by logging in a code at their own terminals. Alternatively, a worker at one terminal may transmit directly to a worker at another terminal.

By using a modem and telephone lines, workers at one office may transmit messages to workers at another. Again, messages may be stored for later referral or transmitted directly.

SPECIAL E-MAIL FEATURES

Many E-mail systems now contain some or all of these features.

- **Broadcasting** allows you to transmit a single message to more than one terminal.
- **Gateways** software permits your E-mail system to communicate with another E-mail system.
- **Sorting** capabilities enable you to classify messages by sender, subject matter, and so on.
- **Accessing** international bulletin boards on the internet.

TIPS FOR SUCCESSFUL E-MAIL TRANSMISSION

If you have a computer message system, you may be tempted to use it constantly, since it saves so much time. These tips will help you use your system wisely.

- Remember that long-distance calls cost money. If you are sending a long document far away, E-mail is not the method to use.
- Keep records of your transmissions. Save them to a file.
- Do not use E-mail to send personal messages. It may seem foolproof and private, but that is not necessarily so.

20

Teleconferences

- Basic Teleconference Features
- Special Teleconference Features
- Tips for Successful Teleconferencing

Today's technology enables meetings to take place even when the participants are on different continents. At times you may be asked to participate in an electronic meeting known as a *teleconference.*

BASIC TELECONFERENCE FEATURES

Audio **teleconferences** involve two or more telephones with speakerphone equipment. At a set time, the call is placed to a given number of locations. All participants can then hear the other parties speak, and anyone may speak and be heard. Speakers do not need to use a headset or hold the telephone; they may be heard *via* microphones from any point in the room.

SPECIAL TELECONFERENCE FEATURES

A number of innovations make teleconferencing more and more useful as a substitute for face-to-face meetings.

- **Video teleconferencing** includes video equipment with the sound equipment of an audio teleconference. Participants in a video teleconference can see each other on a monitor as well as hearing each other. Such transmissions require special lines; telephone lines are not adequate for transmission of moving pictures. However, still pictures such as slides and charts may now be transmitted over regular telephone lines by means of freeze-frame or slow-scan video.
- **Electronic blackboards** are another means of transmitting graphics over telephone lines. Participants may write on the board, which transmits their writing to monitors at the other locations.
- **Computer conferencing** is done with modems and special software. Participants communicate from one computer terminal to another, and any number of terminals may be included.

TIPS FOR SUCCESSFUL TELECONFERENCING

One helpful element of teleconferences is the fact that all data received is recorded. This makes note taking at a teleconference quite simple. You may simply watch and listen and transcribe the conversation in written form at a later time. Here are some other tips.

- Have any supplementary equipment—computers, faxes, cameras, and so on—switched on and ready at the appointed time.
- Arrange seats so that everyone can see the monitor.

- If possible, select one person to input data or write on the electronic blackboard so that you do not waste time moving around and changing seats.
- Make sure any visual aids you use are clear and simple so that they can be easily read off a monitor.
- Speak clearly and do not interrupt.

IV

Managing Information

21

Filing Systems

- Alphabetical Filing Systems
- Rules for Alphabetizing
- Numerical Filing Systems
- Non-Paper Filing Systems
- Tips for Successful Filing

The most important rule for successful management of information is: Be consistent. Choose a system for each kind of filing you must do and follow it religiously. If you are moving into an office where a filing system already exists, learn the rules as soon as possible. The more information passes through your office, the more you need a logical system for filing it.

ALPHABETICAL FILING SYSTEMS

In an alphabetical system, all information is filed in ABC order. There are several types of alphabetical systems.

- **Alphabetical by Name** is the system to use if you are managing a doctor's office, working for the Dean of Students, or organizing any type of business that involves clients. You may organize your system by a person's last name, by first name of corporation, by case name, and so on. Under N, for example, you might list these files.

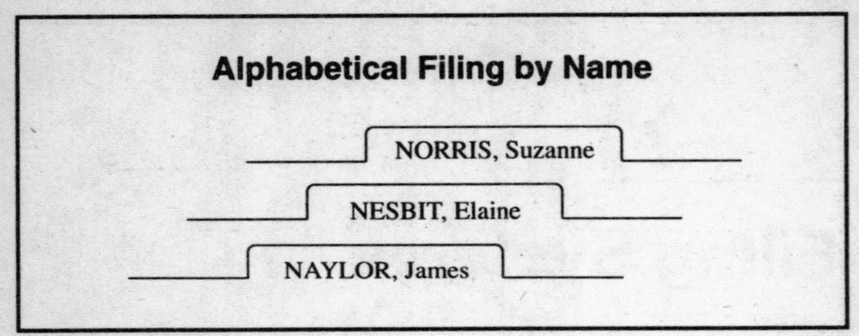

Fig. 21.1

• **Alphabetical by Location** is helpful if you work with a number of branch offices or have sales regions over a broad area. You might list files alphabetically by state or region and then by city within those areas, or by city with clients or companies listed as subheadings. You might even try a combination, as below.

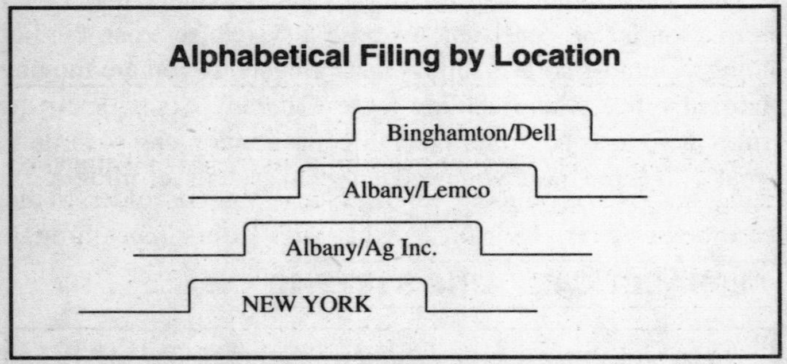

Fig. 21.2

• **Alphabetical by Subject** is useful when the information you are filing corresponds to a number of different topics. You may handle materials for several departments, or your office might deal with a number of products. A subject set-up might look like this.

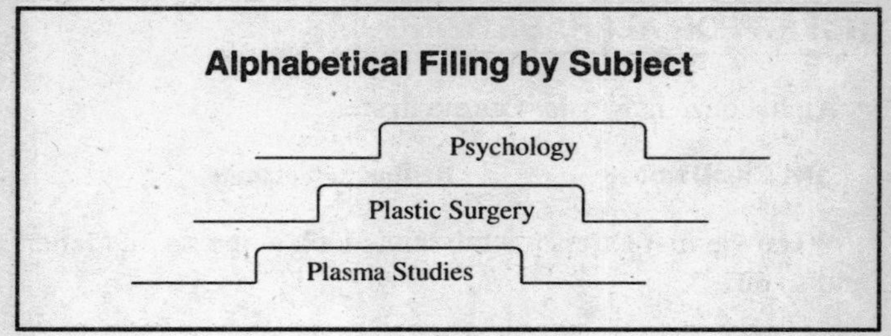

Fig. 21.3

• **Closed-End Alphabetizing** is similar to the guide words on the top of a dictionary page. Everything in a given file folder comes between the letters on the guide.

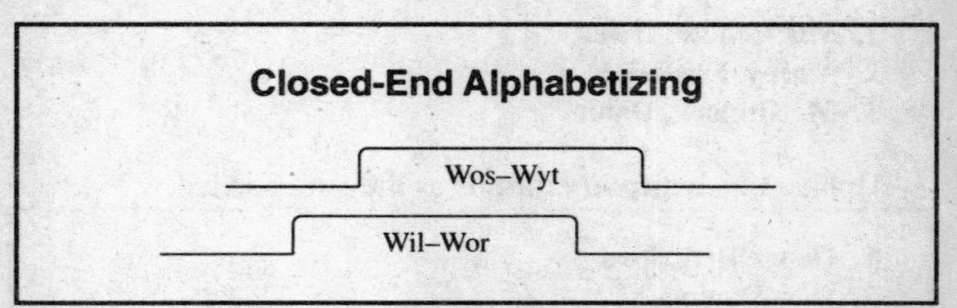

Fig. 21.4

• **Straight Alphabetizing** is similar to closed-end alphabetizing, but there is only one set of guide letters per folder. In the case below, everything that begins with letters *Tem-* through *Tug-* goes in the first folder.

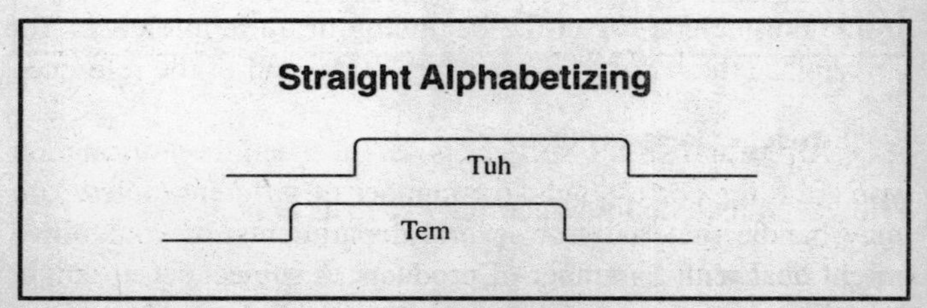

Fig. 21.5

RULES FOR ALPHABETIZING

- Alphabetize names **last name first.**

Del Rio, Damien **Redhook, Norman**

- When the first letters are the same, look at the second letters, and so on.

1. **De**l Rio, Damien
2. **Di**l̲lon, Ken
3. **Di**x̲on, Pamela

- Alphabetize ***Mc*** and ***Mac*** surnames as they are spelled.

1. **MacDonald, Helen**
2. **Marey, Frederick**
3. **McKinnock, Daniel**

- Alphabetize **company names** as they are spelled.

1. **Donnelly & Sons**
2. **Dow-Parsons**
3. **Dox 'n' Sox**

However, a company name that includes the first and last name of an individual is alphabetized by the individual's last name.

Donnelly, Harold, & Sons

- Do not include ***the*** at the beginning of a file reference. You may place the word in parentheses at the end of the reference.

Envelope Company (The)

However, include foreign articles such as *la* or *el.*

El Mirador

• Ignore conjunctions or prepositions when filing alphabetically.

1. **Clyde Foods**
2. **Clyde & Martin**

• Ignore titles and degrees when filing alphabetically. You may include them in parentheses if you wish.

1. **Franklin, Dorothy (Dr.)**
2. **Franklin, Stanley (Ph.D.)**

However, if the title is part of a company name, do use it in filing.

Dr. Dorothy Franklin Institute (The)

• Alphabetize **abbreviations** as though they were written out in full.

1. **Dr. Dorothy Franklin Institute (The)**
2. **Dogmatics, Inc.**

1. **St. Croix**
2. **Saint Michael's Church**

• Alphabetize **digits** as though they were written out in full.

1. **Nexus Club**
2. **99 Club**
3. **Opera Club**

• Ignore apostrophes that follow an *s,* but include apostrophes that precede an *s.*

1. **Sinbad's Cave**
2. **Sinbad Island**

1. **Mermaid's Bay**
2. **Mermaids' Alley**

• Ignore phrases such as *Division of* and *Department of.* You may include them in parentheses if you wish.

1. **Highway Management (Division of)**
2. **Job Training (Department of)**

• When alphabetizing several listings of the same name with different addresses, alphabetize according to city.

1. **Delacorte International, Dallas**
2. **Delacorte International, Denver**
3. **Delacorte International, Honolulu**

• File **governmental material** by major unit first, followed by secondary unit, and so on.

1. **U.S. Government, Health & Human Services**
2. **U.S. Government, Housing & Urban Development**

NUMERICAL FILING SYSTEMS

Depending on the amount and type of information you need to file, you may find that filing by number makes the best sense. There are a few kinds of numerical systems.

• **Consecutive Filing** is useful when filing invoices or numbered forms of any kind. Numbers in consecutive files often begin with 0001 and range to 9999. Some offices assign a code to different subjects or clients and file by code. In those cases, a separate card file should be made, explaining the code system.

• **Terminal Digit Filing** usually indicates the drawer, guide, and folder in which an item is filed. An item numbered 101214 would be located in drawer 14, behind guide 12, in folder 10. It might instead be in drawer 14, in folder 12, as the 10th insert.

• **Middle Digit Filing** is also based on six digits. In this system, an item numbered 101214 would be in drawer 12 as the

14th insert behind guide 10. This system makes it easier to reshuffle paper after files are purged and updated.

• **Chronological Filing** is simply filing by date. This may be useful in a correspondence file or as a record of sales figures. You may set up a folder for each day of a given month and place the folders in guides labeled by month and in drawers labeled by year. Alternatively, you may simply make a new folder for each day when you send correspondence.

NON-PAPER FILING SYSTEMS

In theory, today's electronic offices have less and less paper to file. Materials may be filed on microforms, stored on computer, or filed on optical disks.

• **Micrographics** is the process of storing photographic reductions of documents. Material is photographed in either serialized or unitized form. Serialized microforms are stored on reels, cartridges, or cassettes. Unitized microforms are stored on cards, in jackets, or on microfiche, which can hold several rows of small photographs. The microforms may be enlarged and read with machines called microform readers, and they may even be reprinted original size from the tiny photographs.

• **Computer Files** are part of your software. You can save files to a hard disk, a floppy disk, or a tape. Depending on the software you have, you may have the option of consolidating large amounts of information, merging files, and creating management systems. (For more information on software, see chapter 27. For information about databases, useful storage systems, see chapter 22.)

• **Optical Disks** can store large amounts of information, both printed and graphic. A CD-ROM disk can store nearly a quarter of a million pages of text. Retrieving information from an optical disk is nearly instantaneous, but information, once stored, may not be changed on many optical disk systems.

TIPS FOR SUCCESSFUL FILING

No matter what kind of office you work in, you will need a storage and retrieval system. Here are some tips for establishing and using a filing system successfully.

- Design the simplest possible system that allows you to file what you need to file. Complex systems are difficult to learn and easy to disregard.
- Build flexibility into your system. Leave enough space in drawers or on shelves to add many more files if necessary. It is always better to have half-empty file drawers than to have to reshuffle an entire cabinet full of files to alleviate over-crowding.
- If possible, initiate a check-out system. Have people sign files out and in. If you have people who chronically misfile materials, leave a basket on top of the file cabinet for "material to be filed" and file everything yourself.
- Use cross-referencing when it seems to make sense. If you find that people look for files labeled *Legal* under *Law,* place a paper labeled *Law* in the drawer with a note attached: "See *Legal.*"
- If it helps, use color-coding. Colored folders, colored labels, and colored dots are available, and any of these may help you organize your files. Remember to be consistent about your use of color, however. If you are using yellow dots to designate a particular year, do not switch colors halfway through or use yellow dots elsewhere to designate a particular subject. Your aim here is to clarify your filing system, not to add more layers of procedure.
- It is often helpful to keep an index of guide words. Every time you make a new guide—for example, adding *Biology* to your filing system—make an index card containing that word. Keep the index cards alphabetized in a box on your desk. This

small expenditure of time will ultimately save you hours. It is far easier to look up a word on an index card than to search through a file cabinet. You will know at a glance if something is missing from your files or if you have simply searched for it under the wrong guide word.

22

Databases

- Setting Up Databases
- Types of Databases
- Database Services

Any kind of filing system may be considered a database. A database is merely a set of information and the rules for relating one piece of that information to another. In this chapter, we will discuss databases controlled by and filed on computers. Since there are many kinds of database software, with new kinds being designed every year, we will confine the discussion to general information on database structure. The resource list in Section 6 may help you locate the database software that will work for you.

SETTING UP DATABASES

A database may be organized much like a filing cabinet. What would be a drawer in a filing cabinet is called a *file* in a database. The file card or individual sheet of information in a filing cabinet is called a *record* in a database. Each piece of information on the file card—name, address, and so on—is called a *field* in a database.

To design a database, you must first think about the purpose of your filing system. What kinds of information will you need to retrieve? Will you need to update this information on a regular basis? What specific details are important—names, subjects, addresses, telephone numbers, order numbers, dates? These will become the fields in your system. Thinking about these questions will help you determine what kind of database software you need.

With the right database, you can add, delete, edit, view, compare, sort, and print records. You can search for specific information throughout files at the touch of a key on your keyboard. You can even use information you pull out of records to create new files. For example, you might decide that you wish to search through a file of customers, pull out only those who live in Canada, and place them in a special new file. You might then search through that new file and select only customers who have purchased from you in the last quarter. If you have set up your database correctly, including all the fields you need, you will be able to do this easily.

TYPES OF DATABASES

There are two main types of databases, flat-file and relational.

- **Flat-file Databases** are very simple. They allow you to work within a single file and search for information within that file. An example of a flat-file database might be an address book that expands as more names and addresses are added to your system.
- **Relational Databases** use multiple files that are automatically cross-referenced by the database system. You set up a relational database by organizing a series of tables. When two or more tables have a field in common, the information on the tables is automatically "joined," or cross-referenced.

You have witnessed examples of relational databases if you have ever ordered from a catalog company. The operator may ask you for your credit card number. By typing in that number, she or he pulls up a table containing your name and billing address. There is room on that table for the order numbers of the items you request. Those order numbers "join" that table to other tables in the system, allowing the operator to tell at a glance whether the item is available, whether it comes in your size, and how long it might take to ship it to your location.

Some relational databases include a function that allows you to sort through information by subset without creating a new field. In this kind of database, which is sometimes called *object-oriented,* you could easily flag the good customers in your list of customers without having to add a field labeled *good.* When you called up a list of good customers, it would contain all of the information in the customer list—names, addresses, and so on—but only for those customers you had flagged.

DATABASE SERVICES

Many offices subscribe to database services. These may offer anything from stock market reports to airline flight schedules. Many libraries have card catalog databases that you may plug into. Some have databases that provide newspaper and magazine references and abstracts. Such services are rapidly taking the place of print resources such as the *Reader's Guide to Periodical Literature.*

Generally, you tap into databases in one of two ways. You can dial an on-line service using your modem-equipped computer, or you can order databases on CD-ROM products.

A modem allows your computer to talk *via* telephone lines to another computer. You can download (transfer from one device to another) information from the computer database onto your own disk, or you can print it out. Keep in mind that most database services charge for the time expended in your search, as well as charging a monthly fee. A typical monthly fee might be $10, but time charges may run from $10 to well over $100 an hour. You can cut costs by searching efficiently. For example, if you need information on penicillin, look under *penicillin* first. If it is not there, look under *antibiotic* rather than *medicine*. If you need information on Duke Ellington, look under *Ellington,* not *Duke.* In general, most databases will be organized according to standard rules for filing (see Chapter 21).

The following is a small sampling of available on-line database services of special interest to businesspeople.

On-Line Database Services

America Online (800) 827-6364	stock quotes, business news, bulletin boards, E-mail, personal finance, *The New York Times, The Chicago Tribune,* Library of Congress, Smithsonian, travel information
CompuServe (800) 848-8199	stock quotes, business news, E-mail, travel information, news, weather, financial planning
Dialog (800) 334-2564	Moody's Corporate Profiles, TRW Business Credit, Profiles, D&B Donnelly, stock quotes, business news
Delphi (800) 695-4005	news, weather, education, travel information, E-mail, stock quotes
Dow Jones News/ Retrieval (609) 452-1511	*The Wall Street Journal,* Dow Jones News Service, 2,000 publications, business wire, Japan economy, *Financial Times,* Investext, economic indicators
GEnie (800) 638-9636	stock quotes, E-mail, airline reservations, book reviews, Dow Jones News Service, Charles Schwab investments, major daily newspapers
Lexis/Nexis (800) 227-4908	Standard & Poor's, Investext, Predicasts
Microsoft (800) 426-9400	scheduled to go online by the end of 1995
Prodigy (800) PRODIGY	investment ideas, business news, E-mail, stock quotes, Standard & Poor's, Dow Jones News Service, buy/sell recommendations

Fig. 22.1

CD-ROM databases eliminate the fee for on-line time. A CD-ROM electronic book holds up to 100,000 pages of text or 32,000 graphic images. Discs are usually updated monthly, quarterly, or annually, with charges assessed quarterly or annually. A one-time purchase of a disc of reference books such as encyclopedia, atlas, and almanac might run a little over $100, while one that abstracts articles monthly from business publications might cost $2,000 per year. Depending on your office's needs, you may find CD-ROM databases significantly less expensive in the long run than on-line databases.

CD-ROM Databases

ABI/Inform (800) 521-0600	business news from 100 publications
Business Dateline (800) 521-0600	business news from 350 publications
County & City Compendium (202) 393-2666	census and economic statistics
Moody's Company Data (800) 955-8080	data on 10,000 U.S. businesses
PhoneDisc Quick Ref+ (617) 639-2900	phone numbers of 250,000 businesses and organizations

Fig. 22.2

23

Bookkeeping and Financial Records

- Types of Business Records
- Banking
- Billing
- Petty Cash
- Payroll

Bookkeeping is the organization and handling of financial information. In a large company, finances may be handled by specialized departments. Even the biggest corporation, however, may require you to keep track of your own expenses. The smaller your company, the more likely it is that you will be involved with the financial end of the business. Office assistants may be called on to assist in keeping records, banking, managing petty cash funds, or handling payroll. A rudimentary understanding of bookkeeping can help you tremendously on the job.

TYPES OF BUSINESS RECORDS

Much bookkeeping nowadays is done on computer. (See Chapter 27 for a discussion of spreadsheet software and other computer adjuncts that can help organize your financial records.)

Most bookkeeping systems begin with a journal entry. Such entries are then "posted" to a ledger and adjusted for later recording in a financial statement.

• **Journals** are essentially diaries of transactions. They may contain information from invoices, sales slips, checks, and so on. Usually, each entry is recorded twice, once as a credit to one account and once as a debit to another account.

Financial Terms and Examples

ASSETS:	accounts receivable, cash, inventory, supplies, buildings and grounds
LIABILITIES:	accounts payable, payroll, mortgages, outstanding loans
EXPENSES:	costs of doing business
REVENUES:	money from sales or services

Fig. 23.1

The rule to remember is that assets and expenses increase with debits, whereas liabilities and revenues increase with credits. If you recorded a cash sale of $500, for example, you would record $500 under credit, because a sale is a revenue. You would also record $500 under debit, because cash is an asset. This double-entry system of recording transactions allows you to check your work easily by comparing credits to debits.

• **Ledgers** are a more formal second step in the bookkeeping process. Here transactions are recorded according to type. The "posting reference," or "P.R.," is usually a page number from the journal for cross-referencing purposes.

Sample Ledger Entries

ACCOUNT *Supplies* ACCOUNT NO. *10*

DATE	ITEM	P.R.	DEBIT	DATE	ITEM	P.R.	CREDIT
1994 *Sept 1*		*J 1*	*1300.00*				

ACCOUNT *Arnold Realty Inc.* ACCOUNT NO. *28*

DATE	ITEM	P.R.	DEBIT	DATE	ITEM	P.R.	CREDIT
				1994 *Sept 1*		*J 1*	*935.40*

Fig. 23.2

• **Financial Statements** take all the recorded data from ledgers and report profits and losses over a given fiscal period. An **operating statement** reports income and expenses; a **balance sheet** reports assets and liabilities.

BANKING

Every employee with access to the company bank account must file a signature card with the bank. This enables employees to use company checks or make deposits and withdrawals.

• **Bank Deposits** begin with the filling out of a deposit slip. Usually these are preprinted with the company name.

Endorse each check to be deposited. Your company may have a preprinted stamp for this purpose. Your endorsement, which goes across one side of the back of the check, will usually include the name and number of your company account and the words "For deposit only."

Large amounts of cash or checks may be deposited using special locked bags provided by the bank. Place these in the bank's night deposit slot or take them directly to the bank during working hours. Do not mail deposits that include cash.

- **Bank Statements** are sent from the bank on a regular basis, usually monthly or quarterly. Along with the statement, you will receive all the canceled checks from that time period. These are checks written on your company account, and they must be reconciled with the company checkbook. You may also wish to compare canceled checks and bank statements with information in your ledgers, just to double check your figures.

Organize the cancelled checks in numerical order. Review the statement, making sure that all deposits recorded in the checkbook for that time period appear on the statement. Then compare each check listed to the deductions in the checkbook. Some checks may not have been returned to your bank yet; keep this in mind as you compare the figures. In addition, the total in the statement may reflect interest that has been added and fees that have been subtracted. You will have to add and subtract these figures from the total in the checkbook as well. Banks do make errors; if it is your job to reconcile the statement, you are responsible for spotting them.

Call the bank immediately if you think that they have made a mistake. The bank will check its figures and give you a report. If, on the other hand, the figures agree, go ahead and file the canceled checks with the statement.

BILLING

Assets may be increased through billing. Prompt payment from your clients and customers can help ensure that the balance between your expenses and revenues remains steady.

Mail invoices to clients and customers as soon as possible following a purchase or service rendered. Your company may have a certain time of month when all invoices are mailed; make sure every transaction up to that date is included in the mailing.

Keep copies of invoices with your accounts receivable ledger. If you expect payment within a given time, say 30 days, file one copy of the invoice in a chronological file. Remove invoices from this file as they are paid. When the 30-day deadline is reached, mail a second bill—a reminder—to all the clients or customers whose invoices remain in the chronological file.

Computer programs are available to aid with billing. Such programs provide immediate answers to the question: Who has paid and who is delinquent? (See Chapter 27 for more information on software.)

PETTY CASH

Writing checks for small amounts costs money and wastes energy. Everyday purchases may be handled through a petty-cash fund. This fund may be available to everyone in the office or to a select few workers. Either way, use of the fund must be controlled through petty-cash slips.

Start with a given amount in the fund; for example, $100. As each person dips into the fund to make a purchase, he or she should fill out a slip, attach it to any sales slip or receipt from the purchase, and drop both into the petty-cash box.

Petty-Cash Slip

RECEIVED FROM PETTY CASH

Date __________ No. ______

Amount ______________
Paid to ____
For ____

Change returned to petty cash __________________________

Signature ____________________

Fig. 23.3

At the end of the week or month, total the slips and count the change that remains in the fund. At all times, the total amount from the slips plus the amount left in the box should equal $100. As the fund runs low, add money to it from the company account to make it equal $100 again. Record the credits and debits to petty cash in a journal dedicated to this purpose. This will allow you to keep track of these minor expenditures, which can add up over a year and will certainly affect your financial statements.

PAYROLL

As you saw above, payroll is a big part of the liability side of a company's financial equation. Companies must keep records of wages and salaries, time worked, and tax information. Some companies hire outside personnel to manage payroll and other accounting jobs. Others have separate, computerized departments. Smaller companies may have a single person to handle payroll.

• **Payroll Records** include records of hours for wage-earning employees; lists of data for each employee (including Social Security number, number of exemptions, names, addresses, and so on); and gross wages or salary. Wages are determined based on the number of hours worked in a pay period times the hourly rate. Salaries do not depend on hours worked. They are determined based on a yearly figure divided by the number of pay periods in a year. This example shows how you might set up an employee record for a wage-earner.

Wage-Earner's Employee Compensation Record

EMPLOYEE RECORD: Pay Period Ending

NAME ____________ SOC. SEC. NO. ____________
ADDRESS ____________ DATE OF BIRTH ____________
PHONE ____________ NO. OF EXEMPTIONS ________
RATE OF PAY _____/hr

Hours Worked							Earnings		Deductions			
S	M	T	W	Th	F	S	Regular	Overtime	FICA	Fed.	State	Insurance

Fig. 23.4

• **Payroll Deductions** are withheld by the company from employees' paychecks. Deductions for union dues or insurance are submitted by the company directly to the union or insurance company. Deductions for federal and state taxes are submitted by the company directly to the government. The amount to deduct is determined by comparing employees' gross earnings to tables supplied by the government. Here are some types of deductions.

Federal Income Tax withholdings depend on the employee's earnings, marital status, and allowable exemptions.

State and Local Income Tax withholdings depend on the variables above and the employee's address. Some areas have city taxes, some have county taxes, and a few have no income taxes at all.

FICA Tax withholdings are equal to an amount paid by the company for each employee. This tax covers Social Security, Medicare, and disability payments. As with any withheld tax, the FICA amount withheld from employees is considered a liability. The matching, company-supplied amount paid into the FICA fund for each employee is an expense, part of the cost of doing business.

Unemployment Tax withholdings vary from state to state. Some states require the company to pay the entire amount as an expense. Others require the company to pay some fraction of the cost and withhold the rest, as with FICA.

- **Payroll Reporting** on a regular basis is required by law. Some companies are allowed to report withholdings quarterly. Others must report more frequently. This is the time when withheld amounts are submitted to the government. At the end of the year, companies use their payroll records for each employee to complete W-2 forms for all wage-earners and salaried workers. These forms enable employees to prepare their own income tax returns, which are due to the government in April of the following year.

V

Managing Equipment

24

Purchase and Repair

- Determining Your Needs
- Finding a Vendor
- Evaluating Materials
- Negotiating Costs and Contracts

Your company may have an entire department whose only mission is to purchase office equipment. In such a case, your input will be minimal, although you may be asked to evaluate the needs in your own office or division. If there is no such department where you work, you may be more heavily involved in purchasing. The less you know about office equipment, the more daunting the job can seem. Some simple guidelines will help see you through a major purchase.

DETERMINING YOUR NEEDS

You wouldn't buy a car without considering what you need, how much you are willing to spend, and doing a little comparison shopping. Purchasing office equipment requires the same preliminary steps. Before you ever speak to a vendor, make a list. Include

- the main job you want the equipment to do
- the number of people who will use the equipment

- your office's plans for the future and how they might affect equipment use
- options you might like to add if the cost is right
- training, support, and service you might need
- an approximate dollar amount you are willing to spend
- the timeframe during which you must purchase the equipment

This list will help you sort through the wide variety of options open to you. It will provide a resource to refer to when you talk to vendors. List your needs as specifically as possible; for example, "I want this copier to make double-sided copies and collate. It needs to make up to 750 copies a day." Do not worry about machinery specifications—the number of megabytes a computer holds, for example. State your needs simply: "This computer needs to hold all of our invoices for a year plus daily correspondence and personnel files."

FINDING A VENDOR

Ask around, just as you would when purchasing something for your home. Talk to other businesspeople, especially those whose business needs are similar to your own. Search catalogs for equipment that seems to fit your list of needs. Visit trade shows and dealership showrooms. Ask questions of the salespeople you meet, and take brochures and other literature they offer.

Compare what you find. Choose a vendor, and ask for an appointment to discuss your needs.

At your meeting, the vendor should listen carefully to your list of needs and ask pertinent questions. Do not talk price here, and do not tell the salesperson your timeframe for purchase. Do not let the salesperson distract you from your goals by belittling your needs or suggesting substitute equipment you don't need.

If you and the salesperson seem to be talking at cross-purposes, move on. There are lots of people out there who will gladly take your business.

The vendor may suggest a demonstration of the equipment. You and anyone who might be involved in the equipment's use should probably attend if the demonstration is at your office. If it is in a showroom, whoever is responsible for purchasing should attend.

For large equipment or systems, the vendor will probably put together a proposal. This should include a response to your list of needs, a description of the equipment, and a breakdown of costs. You may ask for proposals from more than one vendor in order to see who can best meet your needs.

EVALUATING MATERIALS

Watch closely during demonstrations to make sure the equipment performs as you would wish. Never assume that machinery can do a task unless you see it demonstrated. Once you have received one or more proposals from vendors, sit down and answer these questions.

- Does the equipment fulfill the needs of this office?
- Is the price within our means?
- Will the equipment soon be obsolete, or can it be expanded and upgraded?
- Is the manual clear and readable?
- Is there a lifetime warranty?
- Are training and support available if needed?
- Is the service contract reasonable?

NEGOTIATING COSTS AND CONTRACTS

Just as when you buy a car, never assume here that the quoted price is the final price. There is always room for negotiation. If a vendor is inflexible, see another vendor.

If you have done your homework, you will have a good sense of typical asking prices for the sort of equipment you are purchasing. If you feel the vendor's price is out of range, say so, and quote prices you have seen.

If the price is within reason, you still may be able to negotiate. If, for example, you are paying several thousand dollars for a computer system, ask that certain items be supplied free—perhaps applications software, training, or shipping.

Every vendor offers a different contract. Read the fine print, and be ready to fight for what you need. Warranties should be specific, not vague. Anything your vendor agreed to in your earlier discussions should be recapped in writing. Make sure you know exactly how long you will have to wait for repair service. Three hours is reasonable; three days may not be. Make sure that installation and training fit your schedule. Remember: just because it is in writing does not mean it can't be changed. If you need help, have your company's legal department check the contract. The best price break in the world will not help you if your service contract is full of holes.

25

Typewriters and Word Processors

- Electric Typewriters
- Electronic Typewriters
- Dedicated Word Processors
- Computers As Word Processors

When it comes to written communication of any kind, typewriters and word processors are the tools you are likely to use. It is hard to imagine what office life was like before these tools existed. Choosing the right tool and using it correctly will save you countless hours on the job.

ELECTRIC TYPEWRITERS

They are rapidly being replaced by electronic models or word processors, but electric typewriters have their uses. Electric typewriters are conveniently portable compared to most computers, so they can be moved around the office according to need.

Newer electric typewriters have automatic correction keys, and some come with paper feeder attachments. Because they have no memory or storage capacity, electric typewriters will never be as efficient and useful as word processors. However, a good electric typewriter will last for years, making it a good investment in an office where paperwork is important but storing it is not.

ELECTRONIC TYPEWRITERS

An electronic typewriter is an electric typewriter with memory chips. You can expand the memory on many electronic typewriters by adding chips or using diskettes. Most electronic typewriters also have single- or multiple-line displays, so that you can see what you have input, move around in it, and correct it, just as you would on a computer. You can block words or lines of text and move them, copy them, or delete them. You can set up columns easily or program in the parameters of your preprinted forms, making them easy to type. Many electronic typewriters allow you to mail merge, automatically adding names and addresses to multiple copies of a letter. Fancier electronic typewriters include thesauruses and spell checkers.

Like electric typewriters, electronic typewriters are portable and comparatively inexpensive, although servicing them may cost a lot. They allow you to make simple revisions of your text, but computers or dedicated word processors are better for composing and editing.

DEDICATED WORD PROCESSORS

A computer that is programmed exclusively for word processing is a dedicated word processor. Its hardware includes a small computer monitor, a keyboard, one or two disk drives, and a printer. Usually a dedicated word processor comes with its own limited software. Since the software is specially designed for word processing, it is often fairly intricate. A good dedicated word processor allows you to edit on a split screen, do spreadsheets, design forms, and perform other sophisticated operations in addition to composing, editing, and printing materials.

Many offices have a shared system of word processors, which may be connected to a single printer or to a single central processing unit (CPU). When word processors share a CPU, they cannot work independently. You may use your processor to prepare letters or forms, but they will ultimately be stored in the shared CPU.

COMPUTERS AS WORD PROCESSORS

If your office needs include more than simple word processing—for example, graphics, database management, or communications networking—you will probably find a system of computers more useful than one of dedicated word processors. (Types of computers are discussed in depth in Chapter 26. Many software programs are available for word processing; some are reviewed in Chapter 27.)

Just as you would for any piece of office equipment, assess your office needs before buying word processing software, and buy the software that best suits you now and will expand to fit future needs as well.

26

Computers

- Types of Computers
- The CPU
- Peripherals
- Networks

We once thought that being computer literate meant being able to program a computer. Today's computers are so easy to use, so "user-friendly," that very little skill with or understanding of the machines and their programming is really required. A minimal knowledge of terms and functions will serve you well, however, in case you need to call a repairperson or order a part. Just as with your automobile, as you learn about the workings of the machine, it becomes less mysterious, and you become a better and wiser consumer.

TYPES OF COMPUTERS

There are three main types of computers with which you may have to deal on the job.

• **Mainframe Computers** process huge amounts of information very quickly. They are generally used to control shared databases and other high-volume applications. Each mainframe can support hundreds of workstations. A bank with numerous branches, a corporation with thousands of employees, or a giant institution such as a university are the kinds of places where you might see a mainframe computer at work.

- **Minicomputers** are smaller than mainframes and larger than microcomputers. They can handle large amounts of information and support several workstations. A mid-sized accounting office, a legal firm, or a small but growing business might house one or more minicomputers.
- **Microcomputers** are the most common computers. They are usually referred to as "desktop" or "personal" computers (PCs). Despite their original role as home computers, they have infiltrated businesses and organizations of all kinds. They may be connected to a network or used independently. It is now possible to expand the memory of most microcomputers, and innovations in software make nearly every conceivable application possible.

Desktop microcomputers fit on top of a desk. Many companies have word processing departments with row after row of desks, each sporting its own computer.

Portable computers come in various sizes. The largest are *transportables,* which weigh perhaps 20 pounds. The most useful and fastest growing line of portables are *laptops,* which fit into a small briefcase and may be carried to meetings and on planes. The lightest laptops are called *notebooks* and on average weigh less than five pounds. The newest, tiniest portables, *personal desk assistants,* are handheld and can translate handwriting into printed text.

Microcomputers, the computers you will use most often, consist of hardware and software. The hardware is the machine itself and its components. The software is the information that tells the computer what to do.

THE CPU

A Central Processing Unit (CPU) controls the system. It stores and manipulates data *via* a board made up of microprocessor chips. The computer has two kinds of memory, *read-only* (ROM) and *random-access* (RAM). ROM holds all the instructions that control the action of the computer—its start-up, its storage, its output, and its interaction with peripherals such as the printer. When you buy a computer, the ROM is usually already permanently installed. RAM is temporary memory. The amount of RAM you have in your computer controls the amount of material you can work with and store. Memory is measured in *kilobytes* (K), which are equivalent to a little over 1,000 characters.

PERIPHERALS

Besides the basic CPU, you will need some form of data storage, some form of input device, a monitor, and a printer. You may also want a device that enables you to access information from other computers or networks; for example, a modem or a CD-ROM drive.

- **Data Storage** is available in many forms.

A **floppy disk** or a **microfloppy disk** inserts into a disk drive attached to your CPU.

A **hard disk** or an **optical disk** stores much more than a floppy disk and is far more durable and permanent.

Various forms of **magnetic tape** are often used for storing multiple pages of text and backing up material from a hard disk. **CD-ROMs** can store large amounts of text, sound, and images.

- **Input Devices** help you talk to the computer.

A **keyboard** is the most common input device. It resembles a typewriter keyboard but has additional command keys and cursor keys that allow you to move around quickly on the screen.

A **light pen,** touched to the screen, can move or modify images on the screen.

A **mouse** is a handheld input device that you roll along a pad to move the cursor around the screen. Commands appear on the screen rather than on the keyboard, and you depress a button on the mouse to choose your command.

A **scanner** is a device that scrolls along a graphic image, digitizes it (translates it into electronic impulses), and transmits it to the screen.

Some computers respond to *voice* or *touch* input.

• **Monitors** are screens similar to television screens. They are available in a variety of sizes. For your needs, a partial-page screen may be adequate, but consider a full-page or dual-page screen if it makes a difference in your line of work. Screens and their text displays come in different colors. The color and resolution can make a great difference to your eyes, so choose your monitor carefully if you are shopping for a computer. Full-page, black-and-white monitors are best for word processing. When the computer is on, the screen shows you your input as well as many of the computer's commands.

• **Printers** come in many types and speeds. The quality and speed of printing will be your main considerations when you choose a printer.

Daisy-wheel printers have a spoked wheel with a character at the end of each spoke. The wheel rotates, and the character hits ribbon against paper, just as in many electric typewriters. These printers are slow, but the results are letter-quality.

Dot-matrix printers hit pins against a ribbon, producing a character on paper made up of tiny dots. The more pins, the tinier the dots, and the better the type quality.

Ink-jet printers use small nozzles that spray drops of ink to form letters. These printers are silent and relatively fast, but the ink does occasionally smear.

Laser printers are the fastest and highest-quality printers available, and they are therefore the most expensive. They are similar to photocopiers in the way they operate. (Laser printers are discussed further in Chapter 29.)

• **Modems** let one computer communicate with another over telephone lines. In order for modems to communicate, both must have the same *modulation protocol.* If you use a modem simply to send E-mail messages, 2,400 bits per second (bps) is a reasonable modulation speed. If you need to transfer enormous amounts of data, you may need as much as 14,400 bps. The difference in speed is dramatic. Nowadays, standard modems average around 9,600 bps, but speed is increasing and costs are coming down. Some modems are equipped with fax capabilities (see Chapter 18). These allow you to fax directly from the computer without printing out first. You can use a modem to call up on-line database services, as long as your modem is compatible with the service you want.

• **CD-ROM Drives** play compact discs, allowing your computer to access text, audio, and video. In addition to the drive, you will need a sound card (unless your computer has sound built in) and speakers or headphones. CD-ROM discs hold around 650 megabytes of information, which makes them extremely useful for data storage (see above). In addition, a CD-ROM drive will enable you to tap into CD-ROM databases (see Chapter 22). One drawback to CD-ROM is its slow speed, but innovations continue to speed up information access.

NETWORKS

A computer network connects several computers electronically. Local Area Networks (LANs) link a series of workstations to a central information bank, or *server,* which manages the flow of information. Workstations may communicate with each other by passing information through the central server, or they may be connected to each other as well as to the server. Included in the network might be a variety of PCs, printers, facsimile machines, telephones, word processors, and teleconferencing equipment.

Networks allow you to transfer documents electronically from one machine to another. They enable you to communicate directly with other computer users *via* electronic mail. This means that a single printer or fax machine may be shared by all the workers in an office, even though each person is working on a different project at a different computer workstation.

Networks vary in their size and speed of transmission, and they may be set up in many possible configurations. If your office is large enough, you may have a network specialist in charge of this arrangement. Nevertheless, understanding the network or networks used by your company can help you take maximum advantage of the new technology, which can simplify your job enormously.

27

Word Processing and Other Software

- Word Processing Software
- Graphics Software
- Financial Software
- Spreadsheet Software
- Communications Software
- Database Software
- Desktop Publishing Software
- Integrated Software

Software tells your computer hardware what to do. Software programs are written in computer language. Most come in a variety of versions, each adapted to a certain kind of computer. All software comes with its own manual. For some kinds of software, especially word processing software, it is often worthwhile to shop around for an additional how-to manual. It is foolish to spend a lot of money on a program and then fail to use it to the fullest because you do not understand it. A well-written how-to manual can be your guide and support, showing you how to use your software to simplify your working life.

WORD PROCESSING SOFTWARE

This is the most popular kind of software. Word processing software allows you to write, revise, format, and print text. No two word processing programs are alike. You may need to do some comparative shopping to find the program that is right for your needs. WordPerfect, Microsoft Word, and Xywrite are just three of the most popular programs. Be aware that once you buy a program, you may often send for free updates as new product comes out. Here are some features contained in most word processing programs.

• **Cut-and-Paste** capabilities allow you to select a piece of text and copy, delete, or move it.

• **Macros** help you simplify repetitive tasks. A macro is a file you create to take the place of a series of keystrokes. You can make up macros for any kind of boilerplate text, such as a memo heading or a letter closing. You can label formatting choices with a macro, changing margins or setting tabs with a simple keystroke. You can even name directories using a macro and use the macro to move back and forth between directories. The method you use to create a macro will vary from program to program. In WordPerfect, for example, you can replace a long text with two simple keystrokes. This can be temporary—for the life of the file—or permanently embedded in memory.

• **Mail-Merge** is a function that helps you send form letters to many people at once. You make a list of names and addresses and merge that file with the file that contains the form letter.

• **Spell-Checking** lets you compare your spelling to a built-in dictionary of words. Many spell-checkers let you expand the dictionary by adding new words.

• **Style** elements such as boldfacing, italics, subscripts, small capitals, and so on can make a report or letter look professionally printed.

• **Thesaurus** capabilities can be extremely helpful. You can highlight a word and use the thesaurus to look for synonyms. You can then replace your word with a word or term having a more accurate shade of meaning.

GRAPHICS SOFTWARE

If your business requires you to produce images as well as text, graphics software can help. Some computers do not have enough memory to use graphics programs, and some printers are not set up for graphic capabilities. Check your hardware before purchasing software.

• **Business Graphics** include graphs, charts, and so on. To make a circle graph of expenses, for example, you might simply enter the data. The program would then convert your entry into circle-graph form.

• **Paint Programs** allow you to create shapes and images on-screen by manipulating a mouse, light pen, or joystick. Depending on the program, you can edit your drawings, add text, scan in photographs or other images, or even animate.

FINANCIAL SOFTWARE

Many companies have software created to fit their specific accounting and financial needs. There are so many programs now available that customized software may not be necessary.

• **Accounts Payable** programs handle invoices from vendors, produce purchase orders, and even issue checks. Most are set up to tell you what needs to be paid when. Many can interact with General Ledger programs to show how the cost of purchases was allocated among accounts.

• **Accounts Receivable** programs issue invoices, adjust payments, specify discounts, and may post income to a General Ledger program.

• **General Ledger** programs handle your accounts just as handwritten ledgers do, but with many time-saving advantages. Most programs will put a credit and debit in the correct column without your having to input the figure twice. Many will give you a running total and will not allow you to enter a figure that is not in balance.

• **Payroll** programs keep track of vacation days and sick days, calculate taxes, generate tax forms, and issue checks. Most payroll software can accommodate commissions, overtime, and other nonstandard compensation.

• **Report Generators** create reports for accountants, executives, and stockholders. They allow you to customize financial reports for varying needs.

SPREADSHEET SOFTWARE

Spreadsheets are worksheets. They can be used for calculating budgets and for other financial planning. A spreadsheet organizes figures and information into columns, say A through H, and rows, say 1 through 20. You locate a "cell" in the spreadsheet by referring to its coordinates; for example, D14. You enter figures or text into cells and then enter formulas and equations that act on those data. As a simple example, picture entering different salaries in A1 through A19 and entering a formula to add them in A20. You might then change A12 to reflect an employee's raise in pay. That change would automatically change the total in A20.

Spreadsheets vary greatly in their complexity. Some hold several million cells. Some allow you to plan in more than two dimensions. These are most often used to forecast sales and budget figures far into the future. Examples of "what-ifs" that a user might like to test are "What if we only made *x* in the year 2000?" "What if our market share increased by *x* percent a year?" "What if we laid off *x* workers each year and allowed people to retire at age 55?" Spreadsheets are invaluable in providing pictures of projected earning and spending.

You move around within these complex grids with a GO TO command. You may also name row and columns with headings that enable you to locate specific cells easily. Many programs allow you to combine spreadsheets for cross-referencing purposes. In the future, spreadsheets will be interactive, anticipating users' "what-ifs" and extrapolating figures with simple commands from the user.

COMMUNICATIONS SOFTWARE

Communications software and a modem can turn your computer into an electronic information center. Different kinds of software can allow you to communicate with other computers, including those at special services such as shopping networks, libraries, and the Dow Jones News/Retrieval Service. (For more on database services, see Chapter 22. For more on modems, see Chapter 26.) Be aware that not all modems work with all communications software.

DATABASE SOFTWARE

Database management systems organize information from simple lists to complete inventories. They act as a filing system, allowing you to cross-reference information and manage your records. (For more on databases, see Chapter 22.)

DESKTOP PUBLISHING SOFTWARE

Word processing programs can produce beautiful text, but desktop publishing programs can design it. With a desktop program, you can design and lay out multicolumn pages, add graphics and text, and end up with a brochure, report, or newsletter as professional-looking as one produced by a printer. A business that generates a lot of publications can save hundreds or even thousands of dollars a year on composition and layout by using a desktop program. You may need additional memory to run a desktop publishing program on your computer.

INTEGRATED SOFTWARE

An integrated package is just what it sounds like—two or more features that work together in one program. A typical integrated program might include word processing and a database or word processing, spreadsheets, and communications capabilities. Obviously, integrated software requires a lot of memory. Many companies use custom-made integrated packages that fulfill their special needs.

28

Dictation Equipment

- Central Systems
- Desktop Systems
- Portable Machines

Traditionally, dictation was taken face-to-face. Nowadays, most dictated material is recorded to be transcribed later. This is much more efficient, since it allows dictation and transcription to take place at workers' convenience. There are a number of kinds of dictation equipment; your office may use more than one kind. When you dictate into a machine, it is vital that you include punctuation, capitalization, and paragraphing, and spell out any technical terms. Soon, your supervisor will be able to dictate into a microphone of a computer. For now, you use a dictation machine that works much like a tape recorder.

CENTRAL SYSTEMS

In a central dictation system, each person who is likely to dictate material to be transcribed has a handset in her or his office. The recording takes place on a central recording device. Usually, such systems are in large corporations that have departments dedicated to word processing and transcription, and the recording device would be connected to that department.

DESKTOP SYSTEMS

A desktop dictation system looks like a telephone; many can double as answering machines. An individual dictates material onto tape and then delivers the tape to a transcriber. Some desktop systems allow more than one person to speak in a kind of conference dictation. Transcribers usually have a foot pedal that stops and starts the tape and allows them to replay dictated material as needed while they type.

PORTABLE MACHINES

Portable dictation machines are often no bigger than a small portable radio. These battery-operated devices allow professionals to dictate material anytime, anywhere. Most use micro- or minicasettes. As in desktop systems, transcribers control the tape with a foot pedal.

29

Copy Machines and Printers

- Types of Photocopiers
- Special Photocopier Features
- Computer Printers

If your job involves paper, you will almost certainly make use of copy machines and printers. Laser printers and analog photocopiers use similar technologies, so it may be helpful to consider them together. In both, light reproduces images on a light-sensitive drum, and the images are then transferred to paper one sheet at a time, using a black powder called **toner.** Other kinds of printers and photocopiers exist and will be discussed as well in this chapter.

TYPES OF PHOTOCOPIERS

All photocopiers work using light. There are two kinds of photocopiers, **analog** and **digital. Analog** technology is explained above. In a **digital** copier, the technology involves a scanner and a printer. Images are scanned into a computer and converted into digital signals.

Photocopiers are classified by speed and capability. If you work in a large corporation with its own duplicating department, you will probably use a high-volume copier, capable of producing up to 100 copies per minute. An individual department might use a medium-volume copier, which can produce up to 50 copies per minute. Low-volume copiers, some of which are desktop models, produce between 10 and 30 copies per minute and might be useful in a two-person legal office or a home business.

Photocopiers have a tremendous number of moving parts, which makes them more liable than most machinery to break down. Make sure you have a solid service contract with your photocopier dealer.

SPECIAL PHOTOCOPIER FEATURES

The more you spend on a photocopier, the more special features you can get. Some of the more popular features are listed below.

- **Automatic Document Feed** allows you to place several sheets to be copied in a tray that feeds them one by one into the machine.
- **Duplexing** allows automatic copying of both sides of a page.
- **Enlarging** functions can enlarge your material by a percentage you indicate.
- **Memory** exists on some models to permit you to enter parameters for common copying jobs. The number of copies run and pagination for a monthly newsletter, for example, could be recalled at the touch of a button.
- **Paper Trays** in some models come in various sizes—8½ × 11, 8½ × 14, and 11 × 14, for example. Some machines let you select a tray by pushing a button.
- **Reduction** functions reduce large materials by a percentage you select in order to fit them on a standard sheet of paper.

- **Sorters** collate pages of multi-page documents into individual bins as they exit the machine.
- **Staplers and Hole-Punchers** staple or punch your finished compilation of pages.

In addition, the new digital photocopiers allow you to edit and alter images before duplicating them.

COMPUTER PRINTERS

Chapter 26 introduced you to several types of computer printers. Basically, printers are either impact or nonimpact, which refers to the way they form letters on the page. Nonimpact printers are the more expensive and are becoming the more popular. They range in the quality of printing and in their capabilities to reproduce graphics. So-called "intelligent" printers combine printer and photocopier in a single machine. They print up to 100 pages a minute from digitized data.

The typefaces available for printers are referred to as **fonts.** Generally fonts are available from three sources: **internal** (already loaded into the printer), **cartridge** (which includes in it the memory your printer needs to print the new fonts), and **soft font,** which downloads from your computer into your printer's existing memory.

Various accessories are available to make printing easier.

- **Envelope Feeders** allow you to feed envelopes from a stack.
- **Forms Tractors** are available for feeding continuous forms through the printer.
- **Sound Covers** muffle the noise from impact printers. They are indispensable in open offices with a lot of printer activity.
- **Sheet Feeders** stack sheets and feed them one at a time. Some models have more than one paper tray to allow you to separate pages of a multi-page document.

To learn more about your individual printer's features, read the documentation that accompanies it. The handbook should be kept in a place where it is easily accessible. You may wish to copy the list of error or service messages given and post the list near the printer. That way, if an error message appears, you will know at a glance what to do to fix the problem.

30

Miscellaneous Supplies

- Paper Products
- Filing Supplies
- Writing Supplies
- Fasteners
- Computer Supplies
- Typewriter, Copy Machine, and Printer Supplies
- The Environmentally-Friendly Office

Your duties may include inventorying and purchasing miscellaneous office supplies. As anyone who has worked in an office knows, nothing is more annoying than running out of pencils, file folders, or correction tape in the middle of a job. Keeping track of supply and demand and ordering supplies well in advance of depletion are skills any office assistant or manager needs. Have in mind the kinds of supplies your office consumes most and watch for bargains or innovations that might improve productivity.

PAPER PRODUCTS

However automated your office might be, you will still consume tons of paper. Most offices have separate recycling bins for a variety of papers one might discard. There are a variety of paper products every office needs.

- **Typing Paper** is classified by content, which means the amount of wood pulp it contains. It comes in different grades, finishes, and weights, all of which affect the price. A *ream* of paper is equal to 500 sheets.

Types of Paper

Content	cotton fiber	bond	sulfite bond
Grade	economy	standard	premium
Finish	smooth	linen	ripple
Weight	given in pounds per ream; 20 is a popular weight		

Fig. 30.1

When it comes to *content,* the higher the cotton content, the better quality the paper. Sulfite bond is used primarily for laser printers or copy machines.

When it comes to *grade,* premium grades are brighter and better for laser printers or copy machines and letterhead stationery because they provide more contrast.

When it comes to *finish,* smooth finishes are best for most purposes. Linen is used for stationery, and ripple may be used for legal documents and certificates. Highly textured finishes are not recommended for use in copy machines or printers. Beware, too, of engraved letterhead; it may not run through a laser printer without smearing.

When it comes to *weight,* look for paper that fits the requirements of your printer or copy machine. Onionskin paper is 9 pounds; kraft envelopes are 28 pounds. Some filing jackets range as high as 40 pounds.

- **Envelopes** come in dozens of sizes. Like typing paper, envelope paper is classified by content, grade, finish, and weight. Sizes are given particular numbers—you might order 500 "number 10 envelopes," for example. Here are some typical choices.

Envelope Sizes

No. 6¾	3⅝ × 6½ inches
No. 9	3⅞ × 8⅞ inches
No. 10	4⅛ × 9½ inches
No. 11	4½ × 10⅜ inches
No. 12	4¾ × 11 inches
No. 14	5 × 11½ inches
catalog mailers	6 × 9 inches
	9 × 12 inches
	10 × 13 inches
	11½ × 14½ inches
	12 × 15½ inches

Fig. 30.2

This is only a sampling of the variety of envelope sizes. Your office will probably need several sizes, with number 10, standard business size, being the most often used. You may need recyclable window envelopes for billing, clasp envelopes for mailing samples, business reply envelopes for orders, interoffice string-and-button envelopes for memos, padded mailers, disk mailers, and so on. The sizes you purchase may be regulated by the capabilities of your printer or typewriter.

• **Labels** come in all sizes and shapes. Sheet or roll address labels may be printed on a typewriter or run off on a copy machine. Shipping labels may appear on continuous rolls that run right through your printer. Some labels are pressure sensitive and self-adhesive; some must be moistened. Some come preprinted with the message you wish or with your return address. Decide how you plan to use your labels—if you wish to type them, you will need a different type of label than if you plan to run them off on a laser printer.

• **Forms** range from bills of lading to invoices to purchase orders to employee records. The kind of forms your office uses depend on the kind of business you do. Preprinted forms save time and look professional. Many are available in continuous-feed form for use with a computer printer with a tractor feed. Most are made from carbonless paper that produces multiple copies with a single recording of data.

• **Fax Paper** may be plain typing paper or rolls of thermal paper. Use the kind of paper recommended in your fax machine manual.

• **Cash Register Rolls, Adding Machine Rolls, and Calculator Rolls** come in different sizes, so check your machine manual. Some rolls are made from carbonless paper, enabling you to receive an instant record of your calculations.

FILING SUPPLIES

File folders, hanging folders, and file boxes are available to make your records management easier.

• **File Folders** come in letter or legal size. They are also available in slightly shorter versions that fit neatly into hanging folders. File folders may be made of heavy paper stock or plastic. The heavier the stock, the more durable the folder, so use heavy stock for folders that will be handled often. Most folders have tabs on which labels may be affixed. Tabs range from full length to one-fifth the length of the folder. You may wish to take advantage of the many colors file folders come in to color-code your filing system. Related to file folders are file jackets, which are closed on three sides to keep materials from falling out.

• **Hanging Folders** hang on rails in filing cabinets. They may be made of heavy paper stock or flexible plastic. Plastic tabs may be affixed to the top of a hanging folder to label the file. Like file folders, hanging files are available in a variety of colors and in letter or legal size.

• **File Boxes** are generally used for long-term storage. They come in a variety of colors and usually have double- or triple-thick sides. Also available for storage of files are expanding files (sometimes called accordion files), plastic desktop file holders, and storage drawers. Purchasing alphabetized file folders can speed the filing process enormously.

WRITING SUPPLIES

No matter how many computers you have in the office, you will still write some things by hand. Most people have personal preferences in writing utensils; keep these in mind as you order supplies.

• **Pencils** may be mechanical or wooden. Mechanical pencil leads come in various widths, measured in millimeters. Wooden pencils are classified according to hardness of the lead. An accounting or drafting office may require an assortment of colored pencils as well as standard pencils. Some colored pencils are easy to erase; others are more permanent.

• **Pens** may be ballpoint, roller ballpoint, nylon tip, or fountain. Different pens are useful for different jobs. Nylon tips are fine for labeling disks but terrible for filling out multiple-page forms. Fountain pens are wonderful for signing papers but far less useful for drawing diagrams. Some ballpoints are retractable; most have caps. Most pens are available in different widths, measured again in millimeters. Typical widths are medium and fine, but extra fine (0.5 mm) and micro fine (0.2 mm) are available in some styles.

• **Markers** include highlighters, permanent markers, overhead transparency pens, art markers, china markers, and easel pad markers. Some markers are erasable. Easel pad markers are designed not to bleed through paper. Some highlighters are designed not to duplicate in copy machines. Permanent markers and china markers are designed to write on a variety of surfaces. The kind of markers you need depend on the kind of business you do.

FASTENERS

If you deal with a lot of paper, you will rely on fasteners to organize it. A typical office needs everything from glue to paper clips.

• **Paper Clips** traditionally come in two sizes, 1¼ inch and 2 inch. Nowadays, however, there are lots of choices. You can use colored, vinyl-covered clips. You can use plastic, non-magnetic clips. You can use paper clamps or binder clips to hold large quantities of paper or files. Each of these comes in several sizes. As with most products, if you buy clips in large quantities, you can save money. Always re-use paper clips. There is no need to throw them away, unless they are no longer functional.

• **Brass Fasteners and Book Rings** are used to fasten hole-punched papers together. The size you require is dictated by the size of the reports or documents you wish to secure. Brass fasteners range from ⅜ inch to 3 inches in length, and book rings are available in a range of diameters, with ¾ inch to 3 inches being typical.

• **Adhesive, Glue, and Rubber Cement** are fasteners your office may need. Spray adhesives are used in paste-up, as are glue sticks. Glues bond all kinds of materials, and some bond in seconds. Rubber cement or paper cement are less messy than glue and allow for repositioning even after the cement has dried.

• **Rubber Bands** come in many sizes and colors. The United States Post Office recommends 3½ × ¼ inch bands for mail sorting.

• **Staples** come in different sizes and shapes and can be applied using standard, automatic, or electric staplers. Heavy-duty staplers can staple through as many as 250 sheets of paper. Clipper staplers are used to seal bags. Most standard staplers hold a full strip of 210 staples. Some electric staplers are cartridge-loaded and hold as many as 5,000 staples.

- **Tape** may be invisible, transparent, removable, or double-coated. Some tapes are designed not to duplicate on copy machines. Some are designed to be written or typed on. Most masking tape is flexible and can be easily stripped up again. Package sealing tape, box sealing tape, and strapping tape are used to seal packages. Some brands stick on contact; others must be moistened. Strapping tape is the strongest, because it is reinforced with glass strands.

COMPUTER SUPPLIES

Most of the supplies you will require for your computer are storage devices—disks, cartridges, and so on. Also available are cleaning supplies and protective devices.

- **Diskettes** come formatted or unformatted. If you buy unformatted disks, you will need to format them before storing data on them. Diskettes are 3½ inches or 5½ inches, and they hold varying amounts of data, measured in bytes. The kind of diskette you buy depends on the kind of computer you have and the amount of data you wish to save.
- **Data Cartridges** are for backing up data. Cartridges come in different tape widths, from .15 inch to ¼ inch. They come in different lengths, and they come with varying capacities. Again, the kind you choose depends on your office's needs.
- **Air Dusters** are trigger bottles of pressurized air for cleaning keyboards and sensitive parts of equipment.
- **Anti-Glare Filters** remove glare from your CRT screen.
- **Dust Covers** keep your PC, keyboard, or printer free of dust.
- **Screen Cleaning Pads** are static and lint free.
- **Surge Protectors** are recommended to protect sensitive equipment from power spikes or noise on the line.

TYPEWRITER, PRINTER, AND COPY MACHINE SUPPLIES

Typewriter accessories you may need to purchase include brushes and other cleaning products, carbon paper, correction tape or fluid, elements or printwheels, and ribbons. The last two accessories are available for computer printers, too. Some printers and most copy machines use cartridges and toners.

• **Elements and Printwheels** are removable metal balls or wheels, each containing a particular typeface. When you order elements or printwheels, you consider the brand of typewriter or printer you are using, the typeface, and the pitch. *Pitch* refers to the number of horizontal characters per inch. Pica type is 10-pitch; elite type is 12-pitch. Some sample typefaces are shown below.

Sample Typefaces

Courier	ABCDabcd0123
Letter Gothic	ABCDabcd0123
Orator	ABCDABCD0123
Prestige	ABCDabcd0123
Script	*ABCDabcd0123*

Fig. 30.3

• **Ribbons** come in an astonishing variety. Make sure that the ribbon you purchase is designed for your brand of typewriter or printer. For a few cents more, you can often buy ribbon with built-in correction tape. Typewriter ribbons are often advertised as delivering a certain number of *impressions;* that is, letters typed. This number can vary from around 40,000 to 250,000; keep this in mind when you compare ribbon prices.

• **Cartridges** are used instead of ribbons in some printers and most copiers. These complex-looking plastic devices hold the printing material known as *toner.* Cartridges can be expensive, but many can be refilled. Check the estimated number of characters, pages, or copies advertised by the makers of the cartridges, and use these figures to shop for bargains.

THE ENVIRONMENTALLY FRIENDLY OFFICE

Any office assistant today should be familiar with local recycling regulations. If your company does not have a recycling policy, why not plan one yourself and promote it at your next staff meeting? It's easy to replace wastebaskets with recycling bins, and you will find that much of what you use in the office can be recycled, from scrap paper to soda cans. In addition to recycling, encourage conservation and reuse. If people in your office copy multiple-page documents on both sides of the paper instead of just a single side, they can save 50 percent in paper costs and eliminate waste. If the office supplies washable ceramic mugs for coffee breaks or asks workers to bring mugs from home instead of using styrofoam cups, a real savings can be had, and more waste can be eliminated. Don't throw things away—reuse paper clips, file folders, supply boxes, binders, interoffice envelopes, and so on.

Most of the major manufacturers of office supplies now offer recycled products. The term refers to products that include previously used material or material formed as waste in other manufacturing processes. Examples include recycled file folders, recycled message forms, recycled colored copy machine paper, recycled ring binders, recycled envelopes, and even recycled stick-on notes. It comes down to simple supply-and-demand theory: As more offices switch to using recycled products, more materials will be recycled. By using these recycled products, you encourage conservation and help the environment.

VI

List of Resources

This list of agencies, organizations, directories, dictionaries, and other resources is by no means comprehensive. It does include some major reference works and other information you may find useful. Many of the publications are annually updated.

PART I: DUTIES AND RIGHTS

Agencies and Organizations

American Association of Medical Assistants
20 North Wacker St.
Chicago, IL 60606

American Society of Corporate Executives
1270 Avenue of the Americas
New York, NY 10020

Equal Employment Opportunity Commission
1801 L St. NW
Washington, DC 20507

National Association of Executive Secretaries
900 S. Washington St., No. G-13
Falls Church, VA 22046

National Association of Legal Secretaries
2250 East 73rd St.
Tulsa, OK 74136

Professional Secretaries International
10502 NW Ambassador Dr.
P.O. Box 20404
Kansas City, MO 64195

United States Department of Labor
200 Constitution Avenue NW
Washington, DC 20210

Books

Directory of United States Labor Organizations. Lanham, MD: Bureau of National Affairs.

A Technical Assistance Manual on the Employment Provisions (Title I) of the Americans with Disabilities Act. Washington, DC: EEOC.

PART II: COMMUNICATING IN WRITING

Agencies and Organizations

Government Printing Office
732 N. Capitol St. NW
Washington, DC 20401

United States Postal Service
Consumer Affairs
475 L'Enfant Plaza SW
Washington, DC 20260

Books

Black, Henry Campbell. *Black's Law Dictionary.* St. Paul, MN: West Publishing.

Blakiston's Gould Medical Dictionary. New York: McGraw-Hill.

The Chicago Manual of Style. Chicago: University of Chicago Press.

De Sola, Ralph. *Abbreviations Dictionary.* New York: Elsevier.

Directory of Corporate Affiliations. New Providence, NJ: National Register Publishing.

Encyclopedia of Business Information Sources. Detroit: Gale Research.

Fast 5,000 Company Locator. Woburn, MA: Corp Tech.

Howard, Cyril W. H. *Black's Medical Dictionary.* Savage, MD: Barnes & Noble.

International Business Travel and Relocation Directory. Detroit: Gale Research.

International Trade Names Directory. Detroit: Gale Research.

Jordan, Lewis. *The New York Times Manual of Style and Usage.* New York: New York Times Books.

Longman Medical Dictionary. New Brunswick, NJ: Isis/Cleo Press.

McGraw-Hill's Dictionary of Scientific and Technical Terms. New York: McGraw-Hill.

Mossman, Jennifer. *Acronyms, Initialisms, and Abbreviations Dictionary.* Detroit: Gale Research.

National Five Digit ZIP Code and Post Office Directory. Washington, DC: United States Postal Service.

Stedman, Thomas Lathrop. *Stedman's Medical Dictionary.* Baltimore, MD: Williams & Wilkins.

Style Manual. Washington, DC: United States Government Printing Office.

Trade Shows Worldwide: An International Directory of Events, Facilities, and Suppliers. Detroit: Gale Research.

Warriner, John. *English Grammar and Composition.* Harcourt Brace.

PART III: COMMUNICATING ELECTRONICALLY

Books

AT&T Toll-Free 800 Directory. Bridgewater, NJ: AT&T.

Frew, Tim, & The Philip Lief Group. *The National FAX Directory.* New York: Pocket Books.

PART IV: MANAGING INFORMATION

Agencies and Organizations

American Institute of Certified Public Accountants
1211 Avenue of the Americas
New York, NY 10036

Association of Human Resource Systems Professionals
P.O. Box 801646
Dallas, TX 75380

Association of Records Managers and Administrators
4200 Somerset, Suite 215
Prairie Village, KS 66208

Black Data Processing Associates
P.O. Box 7466
Philadelphia, PA 19101

Internal Revenue Service
1111 Constitution Avenue NW
Washington, DC 20224

International Data Base Management Association
10675 Treena St., Suite 103
San Diego, CA 92131

PART V: MANAGING EQUIPMENT

Agencies and Organizations

Consumers Union of the United States
2001 S St. NW, Suite 520
Washington, DC 20009

Books

The Equipment Directory of Audio-Visual, Computer, and Video Products. Fairfax, VA: NAVA/International Communications Industries Association.

LaQuey, Tracy L. *User's Directory of Computer Networks.* Burlington, MA: Digital Press.